BILLIARDS AND SNOOKER
FOR AMATEURS

BY
HORACE LINDRUM
The Famous Professional

WITH A CHAPTER BY
MELBOURNE INMAN

British Library Cataloguing-in-Publication Data
A catalogue record for this book is available from the
British Library

Billiards, Pool and Snooker

Cue sports, also known as billiard sports, are a wide variety of games of skill, generally played with a cue stick, used to strike billiard balls, moving them around a cloth-covered billiards table bounded by rubber cushions. Historically, the umbrella term was billiards. While that familiar name is still employed by some as a generic label for all such games, the word's usage has splintered into more exclusive competing meanings in various parts of the world. For example, in British and Australian English, 'billiards' usually refers exclusively to the game of English billiards, while in American and Canadian English, it is sometimes used to refer to a particular game or class of games, or to all cue games in general, depending upon dialect and context. The World Professional Billiards and Snooker Association (WPBSA) was established in 1968 to regulate the professional game, while the International Billiards and Snooker Federation (IBSF) regulates the amateur games.

There are three major subdivisions of games within cue sports: 'Carom billiards', referring to games played on tables without pockets, typically 10 feet in length, including balkline and straight rail, cushion caroms, three-cushion billiards, artistic billiards and four-ball. 'Pool', covering numerous pocket billiards games generally played on six-pocket tables of 7-, 8-, or 9-foot length, including among others eight-ball (the world's most widely played cue sport), nine-ball, ten-ball, straight pool, one-pocket and bank pool. And 'Snooker / English Billiards'; games played on a billiards table with six pockets called a snooker table (which has dimensions just under 12 ft by 6 ft). Such games are classified entirely separately from pool, based on a separate historical development, as well as a separate culture and terminology that characterize their play. More obscurely, there are games that make use of obstacles and targets, and table-top games played with disks instead of balls.

Billiards has a long and rich history stretching from its inception in the fifteenth century. Legendarily, Mary Queen of Scots was buried wrapped in her much loved billiard table cover in 1586. The sport has been mentioned many times in the works of Shakespeare, including the famous line 'let's to billiards' in *Antony and Cleopatra* (1606-7). There have also been many famous enthusiasts of the sport, including Mozart, Louis XIV of France, Marie Antoinette, Immanuel Kant, Napoleon, Abraham Lincoln and Mark Twain. All cue sports are generally regarded to have evolved into indoor games from outdoor stick-and-ball lawn games (retroactively termed ground billiards), and as such to be related to trucco, croquet and golf, and more distantly to the stickless bocce and balls. The word 'billiard' may have evolved from the French word *billart* or *billette*, meaning 'stick', and a recognizable form of billiards was played outdoors in the 1340s, reminiscent of croquet.

King Louis XI of France (1461–1483) had the first known indoor billiard table, and having further refined and popularised the game, it swiftly spread amongst the French nobility. Early billiard games involved various pieces of additional equipment, including the 'arch' (related to the croquet hoop), 'port' (a different hoop) and 'king' (a pin or skittle near the arch) in the 1770s. However other game variants, relying on the cushions (and eventually on pockets cut into them), were being formed that would go on to play fundamental roles in the development of modern billiards. The early croquet-like games eventually led to the development of the carom or carambole billiards category, what most non-Commonwealth and non-US speakers today mean by the word 'billiards'. These games, which once completely dominated the cue sports world have declined markedly over the last few generations. They were traditionally played with three or sometimes four balls, on a table without holes (and without obstructions or targets in most cases), in which the goal is generally to strike one object ball with a cue ball, then have the cue ball rebound off of one or more of the cushions and strike a second object ball.

Over time, a type of obstacle returned, originally as a hazard and later as a target, in the form of pockets, or holes partly cut into the table bed and partly into the cushions, leading to the rise of pocket billiards, including 'pool' games such as eight-ball, nine-ball and snooker. Today, there are many variations of 'billiards' including Straightline rail, Balkline and Three-chsion billiards.

Two-player or team-games such as 'Eight-ball', where the goal is to pocket all of one's designated group of balls (either stripes vs. solids, or reds vs. yellows, depending upon the equipment), and then pocket the 8 ball in a called pocket, or 'Nine-ball', where the goal is to pocket the 9 ball, through hitting (each time) the lowest-numbered object ball remaining on the table – have become very popular. 'Snooker' is largely played in the United Kingdom; by far the most common cue sport at competitive level, and a major national pastime. It is played in many other countries, although is unpopular in America, where eight-ball and nine-ball dominate, and Latin-America where carom games dominate. The first International Snooker Championship was held in 1927, and it has been held annually since then with few exceptions.

HORACE LINDRUM IN PLAY

An extra-firm bridge where the cueing is awkward

INTRODUCTION

By C. D. Dimsdale*

In talks with Horace Lindrum, whether at the table, with cues in our hands to work out a diagram, or sitting down and discussing theory and practice, I have always been impressed by his understanding of the amateur's point of view. This will, I hope, be reflected, not only in Chapter II, where I got him to talk a little about himself, but in the many practical hints that follow. The important thing for the amateur player, no doubt, is to practise as much as possible, but very often a little more knowledge would make the practice more effective. The suggestion of particular basic shots, useful alike to billiards or snooker players, should be taken seriously if you really do want to improve your game.

Another characteristic of Lindrum's broad outlook is that he will not agree with those people who run down snooker when they want to express a preference for billiards. This point of view, which the older professionals all shared privately, seems to him unjust to snooker. As he implies in Chapter II, it is rather absurd for an amateur billiard player, even a pretty cueist, to scoff at snooker without having been able to master it. Certainly for the majority of us there is difficulty and variety to spare in snooker, however much we may enjoy billiards as well.

The post-war revival of professional tournaments has left no doubt of the continued popularity of snooker, as do the amateur tournaments and the keen play in clubs and pubs.

That greatest of champions, Joe Davis, has done more than anybody else to interest the public in the game, and

* Editor of *How to Play Snooker*, by Stanley Newman

v

his enterprise resulted in the successful experiment of taking a much larger hall than is usual for the Final of the Snooker Championship played in London in May, 1946, with Horace Lindrum as the challenger. It was only in the afternoon session of the last day that Joe Davis secured the frame that gave him a score of 73 to 62 and made it impossible for Lindrum to beat him in the evening session for the best of 145 frames.

The champion was at the peak of his form in that match, breaking several world records, making several breaks of over a hundred, including his 200th century quite early in the match. The quality of Lindrum, who during the war had been away in the Australian army, was shown by the toughness of the match. As Joe said, "Lindrum stood up remarkably well against an avalanche of big breaks, and I think Australia has every reason to be proud of the way he battled against phenomenal scoring, which was probably the best I ever put up." Davis himself had every reason to be pleased, not only at the public interest, but at his success against a brilliant younger opponent. Although he retired in 1947, the post-war re-establishment of the game was signalized by the opening of a new hall for tournament play in Leicester Square where the famous "Thurston's" Hall used to be before the blitzing of London.

After that epoch-making post-war tournament of 1946, Joe Davis received a silver trophy and a cheque for £1000, handed to him by Mr. J. Bissett, chairman of the Billiards Association and Control Council. The ticket receipts in the championship totalled about £10,000. A very promising sign of post-war prospects for first-class professional play, prospects which have already largely materialized, so that some exciting contests may be looked for with new champions, like Donaldson, and others, meeting all comers.

These things have sent my mind back to a warm and sunny day in London before the war. The scene was at Thurston's in Leicester Square (bombed out in the blitzes) which was regarded as the exhibition hall No. 1 for professional play, as was the Burroughs and Watts hall for amateur matches. On that warm spring day a queue of people waited to crowd indoors. You might have thought there was a popular film or play to be seen. A spectator who did not know what was going on might also have been curious to note that the queue consisted almost entirely of men. I myself joined it. As we crept toward the door we could read the announcement of the snooker match to be played between Joe Davis and young Horace Lindrum. It was the "Final" of the year's Professional Championship Tournament.

The importance of the match increased the keenness of the queue, which filled the twisting staircase up to the hall on the next floor, where tickets had to be obtained at a booking office window in an ante-room. It was about a quarter to three, and the match was timed to start at 3 o'clock. The prospective spectators were moving slowly up, stair by stair, when two young men were noticed edging their way with tact and persistence through the crowd and upwards. With memories of war-time and post-war queues for more practical purposes, you can guess that this behaviour was not allowed to go unchallenged. The general sentiment was voiced by a man who refused to squeeze out of the way of the two urgent young men. "You take your turn, same as everybody else!" he said. "Hear, hear!" murmured several voices.

"But we're playing," said the elder of the two. "My name is Davis."

"Well, mine's Napoleon, and my friend here is Horace Lindrum if you want to know!" retorted the sceptical objector. Approving chuckles all around were checked by the sudden exclamation of two members of the crowd who now recognized Joe Davis and the undoubted Horace Lindrum with his delighted grin at what was happening.

The ignorant portion of the British Public was silenced. The players were allowed to edge up the remaining stairs, news of their arrival having passed onwards. Within fifteen minutes we were all supplied with tickets, varying in price from 2s. 5d. to 5s. 9d. (prices which may seem cheap to patrons of the post-war comparable shows). For these charges, which for pre-war days were pretty substantial, the keen crowd had the expectation of $1\frac{1}{2}$ to 2 hours of entertainment on a beautiful spring day in a crowded room with artificial lighting, and most of that confined to the fascinating green cloth of the centrally placed table.

Although a true story, this is also a parable. It illustrates certain unusual features about the most popular of indoor sports. The full house included, as it always does at professional snooker or billiard matches, every degree of expertness and ignorance among the spectators, and samples of nearly all classes. The fact that in the West End such matches are rather expensive for errand boys and window-cleaners alone keeps their numbers down, but you see plenty of factory and workshop hands as well as the blackcoats from offices, members of the services, and fruity old gentlemen from famous clubs, who remember the good old days of John Roberts ("do you mean Senior, or Junior?") and other masters of the ivory ball.

Occasionally a wife or fiancée accompanies the male visitor and has the benefit of his whispered explanations and comments. But with the coming of women pros the feminine interest is beginning to become more indepen-

dent of the menfolk, and though they are still few in numbers, young women who really know the game can be
seen also attending the big matches. At present, however,
the feminine element is still fairly well represented by the
lady I overheard at a billiard match between the late
Tom Newman and Joe Davis. She was watching a
really beautiful run of perfect shots by Joe when she
remarked to her friend: "You know, I'm sure he doesn't
mean half the things that happen. I suppose he's what
you call *fluking*?"

But even male members of the audience who are not
pretty expert may often be at a loss to guess the professional player's intentions from shot to shot. I always
enjoy watching the players when the crowd applauds
loudly some surprising shot that happens to have been
really a fluke. Horace Lindrum's enjoyment is especially
catching, when he can hardly take his next shot for
laughing. He never "pretends" with his audience, which
— apart from his beautiful style—is one reason among
several why, to the discerning members of the public, he
is such an attraction.

For the majority, snooker is likely to remain a better
spectacle than billiards, if only because in snooker there
are 22 balls and a variety of colours on the green cloth.
There is also the fact, which helps so much to keep interest
in an ordinary game by a couple of rabbits, that you
never seem to know what is going to happen next, or just
after. Billiards is no doubt a better game for variety of
strokes, but it is more subtle, can also be more monotonous
for all save the very expert watcher. The state of mind of
many men who go to see a first-class billiard match is
reflected in the anecdote about two friends in a provincial
city who sat through a session of a big match. They were
full of admiration. But as they were leaving, one said
thoughtfully to the other. "But, Ted, this isn't the same

game we play at the Pig and Whistle, surely? They seem to play nearly all the time at one end of the table, but we go everywhere."

Before the war, the County Amateur Championships in Billiards and Snooker, not to mention other high-class amateur tournaments always being held, involved about 50,000 players. Now that they have got into their stride again, the eventual prospect is of even larger entries. Nevertheless the professional matches and exhibition games all over the country do not depend for gate money only on the expert amateurs. Those whom I should call the happy rabbits of the green cloth, and even people who don't play, seem to get caught by the atmosphere of the billiard room.

An important element in the distinctive atmosphere of billiards and snooker is due to the sense of colour, and also of touch. Everybody will agree, perhaps, about the appeal of colour and the effect of the lighting. It is strengthened by the fact that the table should be (and in any serious match, must be) illuminated by strong electric lights above the table totalling at least 350 watts. Usually there are three lamps under the large green shades, arranged at regular intervals down the middle of the table, just high enough for players to avoid knocking the shades when they lean over the table, and also to spread the light evenly to the full extent of the twelve feet of green cloth. The remainder of the room must be comparatively dark, nearly all of the subdued light in a match hall for the audience coming from the radiance that floods the green cloth from underneath the big shades. These shades look blacker by contrast. A weak spot-light glows above the marking-board that shows the scores of the rival players, but the referee remains inconspicuous, like the audience, until he advances close to the table to put a ball back on its spot, to call the score and watch the strokes in a fast passage of nursery-cannons for example, or to scrutinize a position that has been questioned, such as that of a doubtful "free ball" in snooker. The sense of touch which responds to the play is more noticeable to some people than it is to others. When I watch Horace Lindrum sometimes doing smooth, quiet positional shots with a beautiful cue rhythm, it makes me think of velvet.

But undoubtedly it is the lighting of the room that gives a special character to the game, and probably helps the atmosphere of decorum that prevails at important matches. Except for occasional applause, voices are sub-dued, cigarettes and pipes are lit almost furtively, for fear of disturbing a player on his stroke, and the only constant noises are the clicks of the balls, the crash of one driven hard into a pocket, and the referee's calling of the score. The referee can be a personality, a part of the show, almost as much as a conductor can be at an orchestral concert. I wonder who, if anybody, will take the place of the late Charles Chambers, who was marker and referee at Thurston's. No famous professional player could hope to equal his dignity, his decisiveness when giving a verdict, his knowledge of the finer points of the rules. And he could bring out a little joke with the brightest, and on occasion the audience would watch him stroll to the other end of the table opposite to where the reporters sat, and make a soft spoken comment to them with a cynical smile.

While one can enjoy the spectacle and atmosphere of a big match without any expert knowledge, the fact remains that, as in other spectacles involving the highest possible skill, knowledge refines and deepens the observer's pleasure. And though it does not look physically stren-uous, to achieve the greatest feats in billiards and snooker is as much a test of skilled endurance and control as it is in any other game, including golf. I am thinking of such feats as that described in the following Reuter report from Sydney in October, 1945—

Horace Lindrum, nephew of the world-famous Walter Lindrum, created a new world snooker record here when he cleared the table with a break of 144, only three points less than the highest possible.

After his opponent had broken the reds, Lindrum went to the table and sunk all 15, taking 12 blacks and 3 pinks. He then cleared all the colours.

Lindrum, who held the previous record of 141, made in London in 1936, proposes to ask for recognition of his record break.

Actually, the occasion was not recognized as official, though the break was made on a standard table. It should be mentioned also that "the highest possible" could in theory be raised by the first player fouling when attempting to break the reds, so giving the man who clears the board some points for a foul, and the chance of potting a colour as a free ball in place of a red to begin his break. The colour would come up again before the process of clearing the board began.

Lindrum, however, has enough official records to his credit not to worry unduly, and we may expect to hear a lot more of him in first-class play in Britain, as well as in the Dominions. No great player of his age has travelled so widely and played in such a variety of places as has Horace Lindrum. He already has the experience of a veteran. Spectators have some treats in store watching players of his calibre during their best spells on the mahogany-framed slate that is covered with the finest West of England cloth, and edged by resilient rubber cushions.

Play on the billiard table has been refined and made less chancy since slate took the place of wood for the bed of the table, cushion-accuracy has been improved, and composition balls of standard weight and size adopted in place of the old, fascinating ivory ones, which suffered

strange moods with the temperature. The old masters
had their day and some glorious moments, but as in tennis,
golf, and many other games offering the possibility of
the highest skill, mental as well as physical, the standard
has undoubtedly gone up.   But comparisons are difficult,
owing to changed conditions, as the old master of an
earlier generation, Melbourne Inman, explains in the
reminiscences which so happily start this book. His tribute
to the younger player also is in the best tradition of the
game, as well as being thoroughly deserved by Lindrum,
whose past achievements in both billiards and snooker
were largely forgotten by the British public before his
match with the great Joe Davis in 1946 for the Championship had brought him back into our limelight.

 I anticipate some more beautiful play between Lindrum
and our new stars which will thrill the public. It is
strange how we rabbits of the game take the greatest
pleasure in seeing it played perfectly and yet are usually
so lazy about improving our own play. May this little
book stimulate the reader to "go to it." A game that is
worth playing at all is worth playing well, at least as
well as one can play.

CONTENTS

CONTENTS

CHAPTER XI

CHAPTER I

A VETERAN'S TRIBUTE TO YOUTH

By Melbourne Inman

MY journalistic friends are fond of referring to me as "the veteran," and everybody knows what Tom Webster has done to my likeness. I suppose, therefore, I may be allowed to adopt a tone of patriarchal reminiscence in speaking to keen amateurs about young Horace's helpful book.

I first saw a billiard table in 1892, and that was at my father's club at Twickenham ; which is going back a bit, isn't it?

I played my first professional match with John Roberts at the Egyptian Hall, Piccadilly, in 1899. In looking backward, I have no doubt that public attendance at matches is much bigger than it ever was in my early days, and more people play billiards now, not to speak of snooker, than ever before.

John Roberts

John Roberts, in my opinion, was the greatest showman I have ever seen in the game. Not only was he a great player, he was a wonderful personality. When I first played him in 1899, composition balls were just being brought on to the market. I was beaten, never having seen a composition ball before. But after that I played Roberts many games with ivory balls, and he never beat me. But he was a nice player to play against. He never complained about the tools, and so on. The only time I ever heard him go off the deep end was an occasion when the attendance was not good.

Big Breaks

Times have changed. In our game they have changed for the better on the whole. I admire the younger generation of players, and among them I have no doubt —and my opinion is supported by many good judges— that Horace Lindrum has an unrivalled record for his age. In the whole of my career I have never heard of any young player of his age—which was then twenty-four— show such all-round mastery, with breaks of over a thousand at billiards, and in snooker such breaks as his 131 official break and his 135 and 141 unofficial breaks early in 1937, not to speak of his more recent achievements. In my view, when he is not playing so much snooker he will become still greater at billiards than he is already.

So far as billiard breaks are concerned I really think that the modern composition balls are easier than the old ivories to play with. Having had so long a spell of playing with ivory balls I still find it difficult to play with the composition balls, but this does not apply to the young exponents of the game, and in spite of my own handicap I am a believer in the composition ball.

During my career in billiards all kinds of freak shots have been brought out and have duly passed away in the broader interests of the game. Among the early ones that mattered was the spot stroke. Most of the professionals were playing it, and making big breaks with it, but there was only one really great spot stroke player. That was W. J. Peall, who stood out by himself, his record break being 3304.

Then came Reece with the anchor stroke. He first exploited this against your humble servant! That was in 1907, at Thurston's. He made breaks of 1200 and 1800 during the match of 16,000 up for £100 a side. But I saw that really huge breaks might be made with it, and sure enough Reece in an exhibition match later

wound up with a break of 499,000! Hard luck for the half million? But think of the effect upon the game. Wisely this stroke was barred, and a new rule was introduced that after thirty such cannons the player must hit a cushion before scoring another cannon.

Reece then adopted a new stroke, called the pendulum

stroke, which he was said to have discovered, though I have heard that it was in fact discovered by a marker.

Nursery Cannons

By a curious coincidence the pendulum stroke also was first tried out on me by Reece. He at once began making breaks of over 1000 with it, and it was soon barred, causing the rule to be made that after thirty-five cannons the player strikes the object ball first, then a cushion, and cannon. But this did not prevent great cueists from making big runs of nursery cannons, against which fresh legislation was made to check the tendency to monotony. That belongs to our own days, which are so full of fine talent and marked by ever growing popularity for the green table.

But let me now make way for Horace Lindrum. He has much to tell you that should be useful.

CHAPTER II

THE IDEA OF THIS BOOK

You can't get away from the fact that the game of snooker's pool is more popular to-day than billiards. Clubs and saloons tell the same tale as the "gate" at professional tournaments and exhibition matches. That is the experience of myself and the leading professionals whom I have played with in Britain and various parts of the Empire.

Although billiards is the more scientific and varied game, I think the popularity of snooker is a good thing in the long run for billiards. Except for the elementary stages of billiards, which I shall deal with before coming to the main part of this book, the beginner can get on better with snooker. That is to say, he (or she, for women are taking up the game in increasing numbers) can reach the stage of being able to enjoy playing a game more quickly than with billiards.

There are good reasons for this, which will become apparent when the two games are compared. The result is that more people are using the billiard table for recreation than ever before. Many of those who start with snooker and attain a fair amount of skill at it ultimately turn to billiards for its greater variety and subtlety, and the scope it offers for artistry in play.

But do not misunderstand me. Snooker should not be thought of as an inferior sort of game by any amateur who cannot make breaks of 60 to 80. It offers any amount of opportunity for brainy tactics as well as skilful cueing. There is too much merely careless play, and I think it is a great mistake, for instance, to ignore penalties for fouling. There is nothing unfriendly about observing the rules of a game.

Practise Methodically

No amateur need feel discouraged by playing very badly to start with. I can assure you that except for any unavoidable handicap like bad eyesight or paralysis of the arms, there is little difference in natural equipment between the amateur and the professional. The gulf between their standards of play is due almost entirely to the professional's patient practice and concentration. What is a game to the amateur, for spare time recreation, is to the professional a whole-time job. So granted this, what then?

Simply that, within the limits of a recreation, the amateur may adopt the methodical methods of the professional to obtain as much skill as possible. While there is nothing like practice at the table, I hope to prove that the advice of an expert familiar with styles of play all over the world can make a lot of difference to your game.

Too many amateurs continue year after year to knock the balls about without giving any intelligent thought or effort to improving their play, or they get quickly discouraged at failure, simply for want of a little knowledge of the right kind. What I intend to do in the following pages is to make you concentrate on essentials, because a moderate mastery of a few comparatively simple strokes can turn anybody into a good amateur player, by which I mean one who is in the 100 break class in billiards, and the 20 or 30 at snooker.

How I Started

Before coming to practical matters, I will add a word about my own career so far. As I have done pretty well in professional snooker, many people are apt to think of me as essentially a snooker player, but I do not so consider myself.

I started with billiards in Melbourne, when I was twelve, and there was no snooker of importance until after 1918. I was coached a little at first by my grandfather, who kept a saloon with twenty tables, and I remember meeting some of the old stars, including John Roberts, Jun.; the Scottish pro., Tommy Aiken; Stephenson, and Faulkiner. My grandfather had no idea of making me into a professional, and indeed I was soon left to my own devices.

I must have been about thirteen when I began on my own initiative to practise seriously on one of my grandfather's tables. I used to try to model my play on that of my uncle, Fred Lindrum, Jun., and later I improved it on Willie Smith's when I saw him play in Australia.

Still later I saw my Uncle Walter play often, but my game by then was largely formed. I can remember the first big match Walter played. It was against Stephenson, and as was the practice in those days, they played for a total score, 16,000 or 18,000 up, at the rate of 660 each session. The modern time limit is, of course, more convenient for big matches.

In support of my claim to be a billiard man quite as much as a snooker man, I may remind the reader that I was the first to make a break of over a thousand under the new baulk line rules, when I scored 1008 in the 1935 Gold Cup Tournament, and that in the next eighteen months I made a dozen breaks of above a thousand.

And will the earnest amateur who reads this please note, in view of what I have to say later, that when I started I used to practise important simple shots, one of the chief of which was the losing hazard half-ball stroke? Then I tried the various degrees of "screw." But the half-ball stroke was the essential, the only other comparable with it being, naturally, the winning hazard or "pot."

Basic Strokes

Now there is a method in practising, and I shall concentrate on a few basic strokes which must be mastered, without any reference to a particular game. Although the next chapters may seem to be for beginners, probably many amateurs who have played carelessly for years will find them worth perusing before we get any farther.

Beginners should read first the caption opposite Diagram Two, but this will be unnecessary for most readers of this book. Practice in the strokes however will be of benefit to the great majority of snooker or billiard players.

CHAPTER III

POT AND PLAIN HALF-BALL STROKE

WHATEVER stroke you are going to attempt, the desired result will depend first upon how you handle your cue.

There is nothing like watching a good player to help one in forming good habits, but anybody who has watched a number of leading professionals will realize that there can be no hard and fast rules about correct stance, or how to hold the cue. The player's individuality and habit in such matters make up a part of his style.

I am not going to tell you to stand square to the aim, or to stand sideways; nor will I advise anybody to grip the butt of the cue in the palm of the hand, or to hold it between the fingers and thumb.

Even the weight of the cue is largely a matter of habit and personal choice. My own cue is 18 ounces, and I may say that most modern professionals favour cues somewhat heavier than the cues used by most amateurs. If you get on well with a 16½ ounce cue, by all means stick to it.

Cue and Grip

So much for the matters I do not dogmatize about. But all the more attention must be given to the essentials.

One is to keep your own cue and get used to it. If it is a good stick and well balanced, it can become a part of your game, a medium through which your individual style as a player is asserted.

As to holding the cue, the essential is that the hold should be firm enough to prevent any wobbling on the stroke, and for this it is not necessary to adopt the modern style of gripping the butt so that it is tight against the palm of the hand, but many professionals do so and if this suits you, keep to that hold. Do not change about between the palm grip and the hold that I myself, for instance, use; which is to have the fingers half curled round the butt, thumb pressed against the opposite edge, but the butt not touching the palm of my hand, except for some unusual stroke.

Stance

The choice of stance must be governed by comfort, the object being easy cue delivery. For correct aiming the striker should get well down over the cue and not stand in a semi-upright position.

There are players who sight very well from well above the level of the cue, but this applies to only a limited number of strokes, chiefly winning hazards. It is much easier to aim if you sight so that the cue, the cue ball and the object (ball or pocket) stretch ahead of your eyes instead of below.

The essential about cue delivery is that the cue should travel in the line of the aim, and not sideways. If you want to test yourself, the usually recommended exercise is to place the cue ball on the middle spot of the D and try to send it straight up the table, over the blue and black spots so that it strikes the top cushion and comes back and crosses the baulk line near the brown spot, the point of departure. Try the stroke at varying strengths. I have marked in Diagram 2 what I consider allowable deviations from accuracy with a fast stroke, and if you can do the stroke within these limits consecutively, you are propelling the cue pretty well.

Correct Cueing

While practising this exercise the cue ball must be

struck in the centre, and the ability to do this at will is almost as important as the piston-rod forward movement of the cue, which should always follow a little way after the cue ball before being withdrawn with the tip near the cloth.

It is useful to follow up this exercise with another ball on the brown spot, the cue ball being placed a few inches behind it, say at the middle of the curved line of the D. Then aim to send the object ball straight up the table so that it meets the cue ball coming back.

If you can strike centrally at will and send the cue straight, to do the shots in the other diagrams at the end of this chapter, then test your accuracy at potting with the plain ball stroke (i.e. by central striking of the cue ball) in the manner shown in Diagram 5.

Each of the middle pockets should be tried, and from each of the three spots on the baulk line. Play the ball at medium strength, so that the nap of the cloth does not noticeably affect the direction. You will discover, incidentally, that the nearer shoulder of the pocket is the more dangerous one, and that it is safer to aim inside the "bump" of the farther shoulder than at the middle of the pocket, as the size of the ball leaves very little margin for wrong direction. If it should graze the nearer shoulder of the pocket it will not go in. When you can pot nine times out of ten strike cue ball a little higher and let it follow the object-ball into the pocket.

So far these strokes have been solely to test your cueing. If you can aim straight, the desired result should be obtained, *and it must be obtained before you can hope to tackle the essential strokes with confidence.*

The Winning Hazard

One of these is the winning hazard, which you have just been doing in the cue practice. The other is the plain half-ball stroke, by which the most useful kind of losing hazard is made, not to speak of other important shots.

Now study Diagram 6 attentively. It explains the theory of the winning hazard and prepares the way for a mastery of the half-ball stroke.

The ball A in Diagram 6 may be pocketed from any angle between the positions numbered 1 and 7, or even a little farther round than these, nearer to what would be 9 and 3 o'clock on a clock face. If the cue ball is at position No. 4, in a straight line with the middle of the pocket and the object ball, the latter must be struck in the centre to pot it.

Obvious. But not all amateurs have grasped the consequences.

If A is potted by a full ball contact of the cue ball from position No. 4, the dotted circle shows where the cue ball is at the moment of impact, and the centre of that dotted circle marks the centre of the cue ball. But only one point of ball A has been struck, the centre of the side facing No. 4 cue ball.

Now, if you are in positions 1 or 7 and want still to pot ball A, the diagram shows how it is that precisely the same point must be struck on A, although instead of a full ball contact a fine cut has to be made. And when aiming for that fine cut, you will remember to allow for the diameter of the cue ball, so that its centre shall reach the centre of the dotted circle.

Half-Ball Contact

Just as A will travel in a given direction after being struck by the cue ball, the cue ball also obeys a mechanical law and takes a direction after contact with the object ball according to the force and angle of approach, if it has been struck centrally by the tip of the cue. The knowledge of this angle of departure of the cue ball after striking the object ball is exploited in many shots, the chief of which is the losing hazard or "in-off," which is easiest and best for controlled play when the contact is half-ball.

By half-ball contact is meant that the cue ball is seen from the end of the cue as a circle that half eclipses the circle of the object ball; when the stroke is made, the centre of the cue ball is in line with the edge of the object ball. Hence when you aim for a half-ball stroke, the tip of the cue pointed at the centre of the cue ball should also be pointing at the inside edge of the half eclipsed object ball, as shown in Diagram 1.

Later we shall look at various important shots that depend upon this knowledge of how the cue ball comes off the object ball, but the basis of accuracy in all such shots is control over the half-ball contact.

DIAGRAM 1

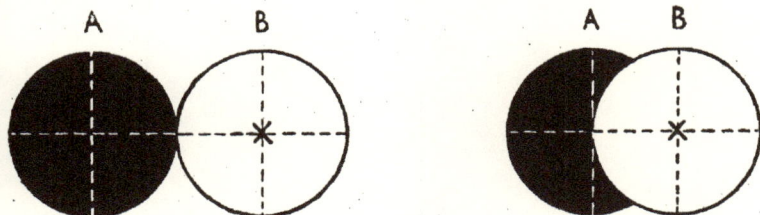

The object ball (A) and the cue ball (B) side by side. If a thin "cut" were being made, the edge of (B) would slightly overlap the edge of (A).

The cue ball (B) half eclipses the object ball when aiming for a half-ball stroke. The cue strikes where the cross is marked. This is the centre of (B) and in line with the edge of (A). The left edge of (B) reaches to the centre of (A).

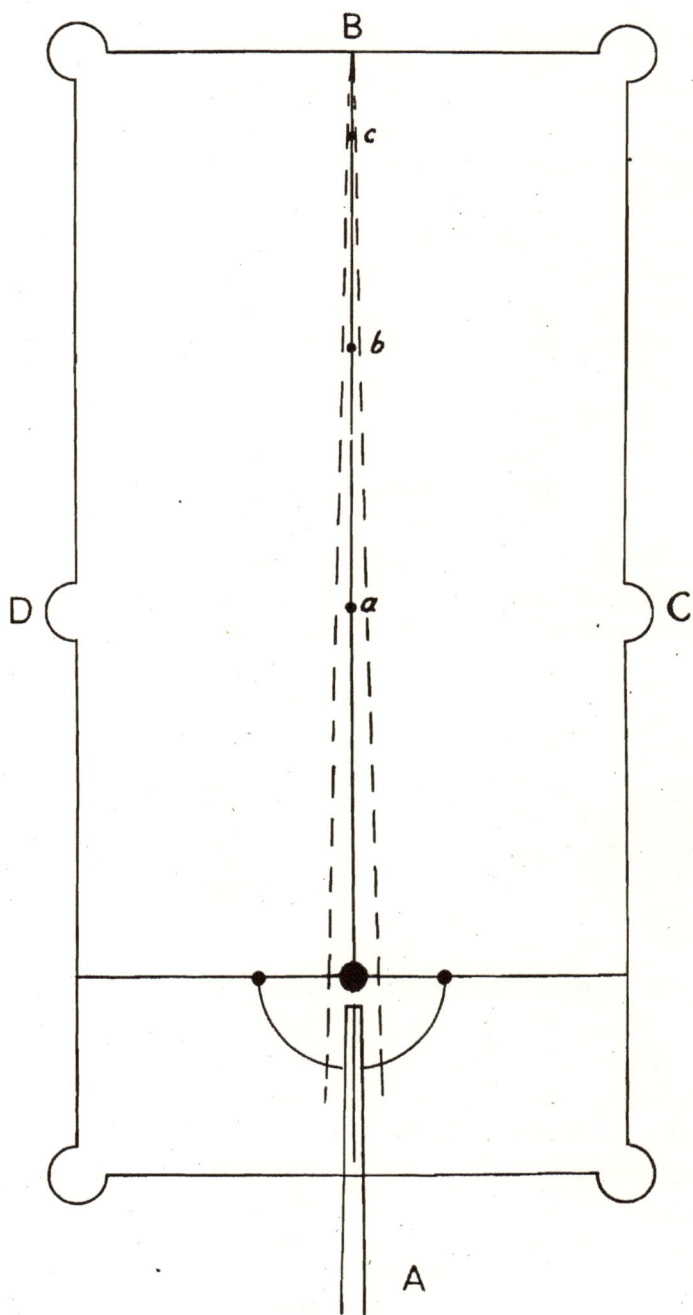

B

D

C

a

b

c

A

14

DIAGRAM 2

EXERCISE TO TEST CUEING

Place cue ball over the brown snooker spot and play it at medium strength (that is just hard enough to bring it back to the bottom cushion). The dotted lines show excusable margin of error for an amateur doing a sequence of such strokes at medium strength.

Key to the table—

A. Bottom.

B. Top.

C. Right Middle Pocket.

D. Left Middle Pocket (similarly the corner pockets are Right and Left Bottom and Right and Left Top Pockets).

The middle of the table is marked by the Brown Spot; the Blue Spot (*a*); the Pyramid or Pink Spot (*b*); and the billiard or Black Spot (*c*).

The nap goes towards top end of table.

Cue ball is the one struck by the cue. *Object ball* is the one struck by the *cue ball*. In snooker a ball *on* is one that can lawfully be played on by the *cue ball*. (The only occasion when two of the colours can be potted with one stroke without fouling is when a "free ball" has been granted owing to the player being wholly or partly snookered after a foul by his opponent. He can nominate a ball to play in place of the ball "on." If he should pot the snookered ball as well as the nominated ball, the nominated ball is merely respotted and he scores the value of the ball "on."

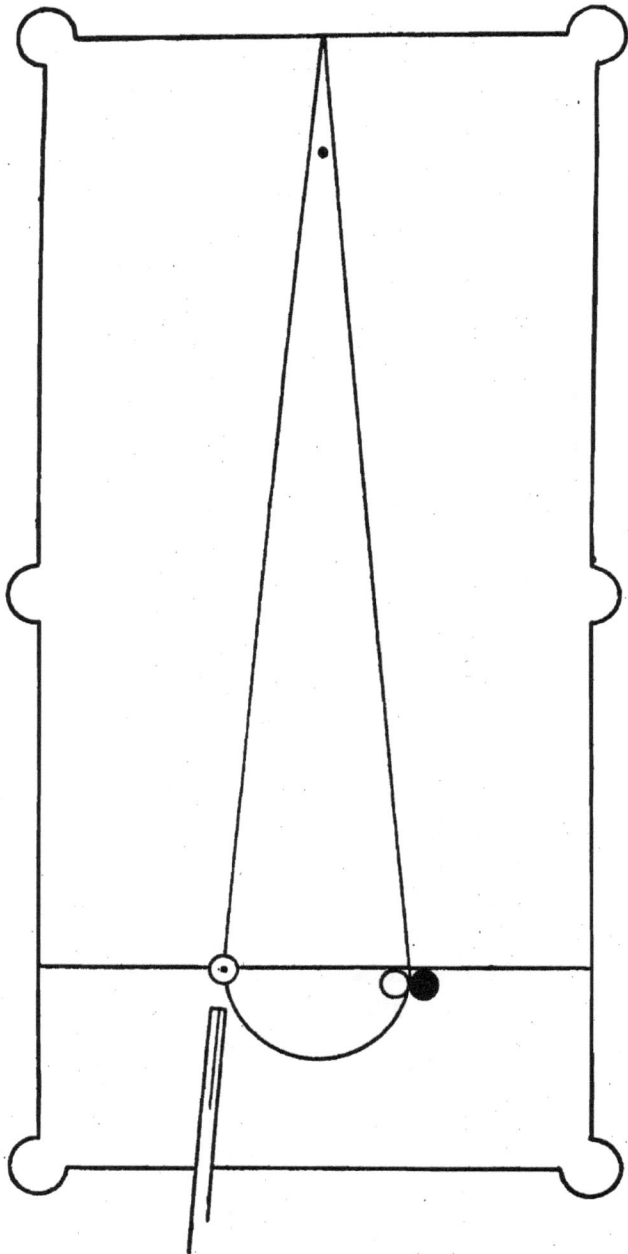

DIAGRAM 3

ANOTHER EXERCISE

Cue ball on outside spot of D, two other balls close to opposite outside spot of D, inside baulk line. Play for cannon off top cushion. It is not difficult to aim for middle of top cushion behind the billiard spot, from which the natural angle of the ball will take it as shown by the line, to the two balls together. But cueing must be true. This stroke off a cushion is useful in snooker. See Diagram 4.

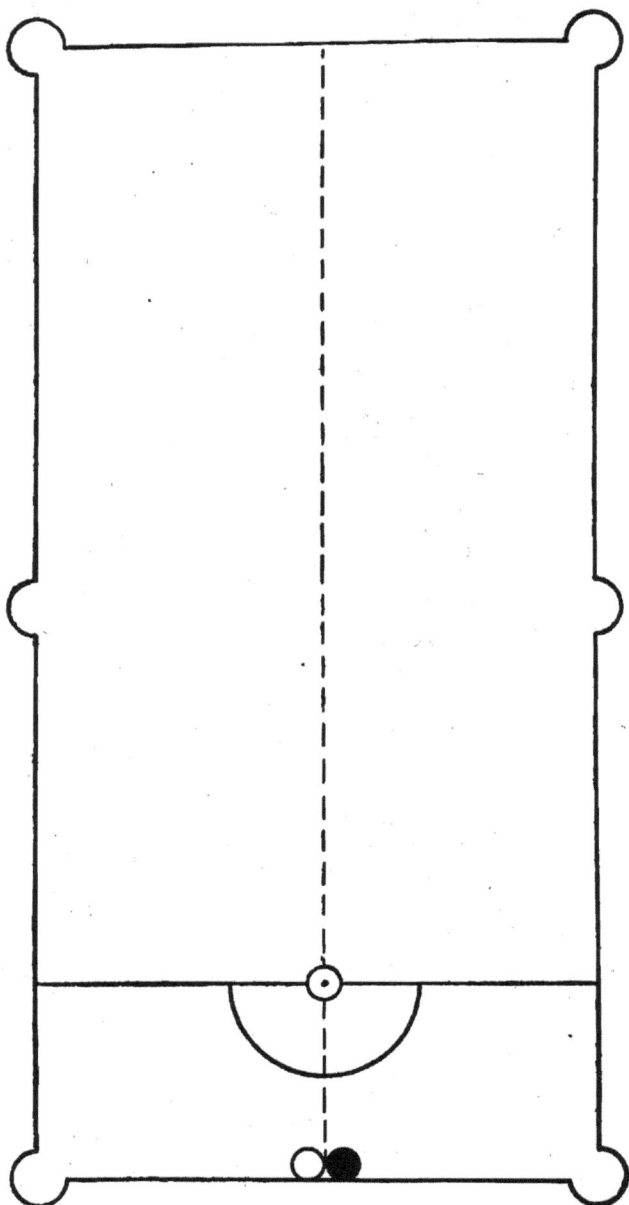

DIAGRAM 4

MORE CUEING PRACTICE

Do this cannon, playing from middle (brown) spot of D to middle of top cushion and straight back to middle of bottom cushion between the two balls there. Only a true stroke without any side will make the cannon, as there is very little margin for error in direction. Try to do it twice in every three strokes..

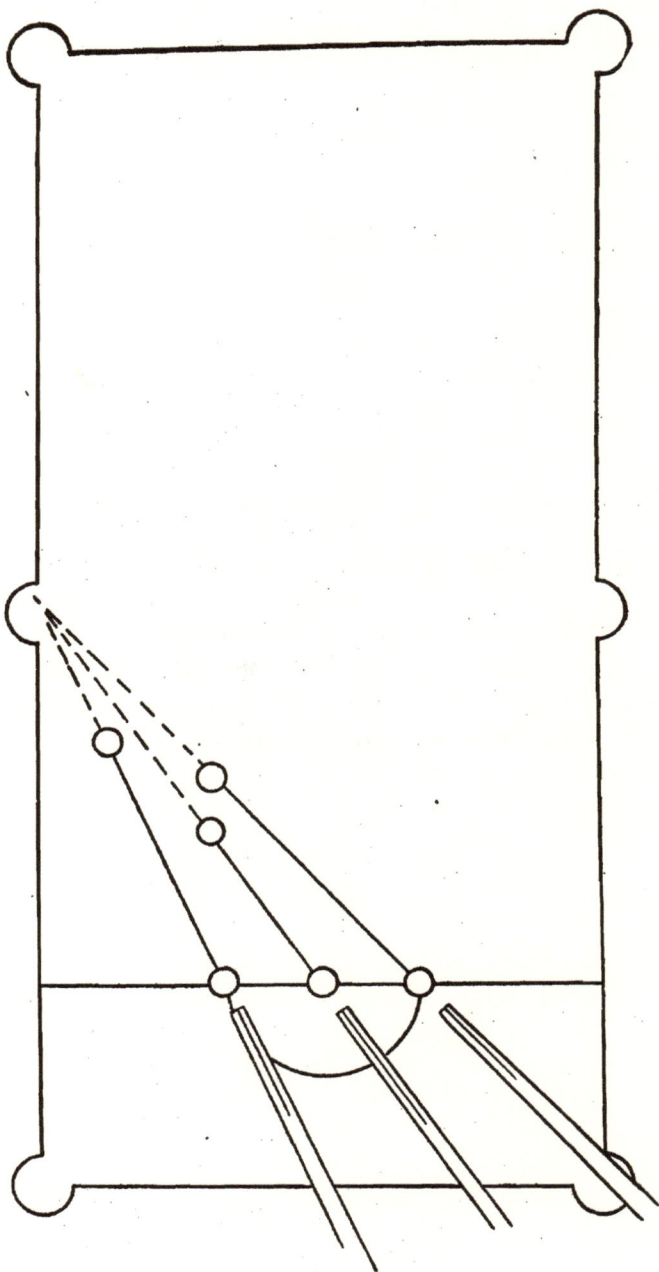

DIAGRAM 5

CUEING AND POTTING EXERCISE

As a further test of straight cueing, place cue ball in turn on each of the baulk line spots, and the object ball anywhere between it and the middle pocket, so that a plain ball stroke will pot the object ball. Take each middle pocket for this exercise, and attend more to the one that seems harder. Most players prefer one side or the other according to whether they are right or left-handed. When you are confident of potting the ball nine times out of ten, try the "six shot" following through, as described on p. 11.

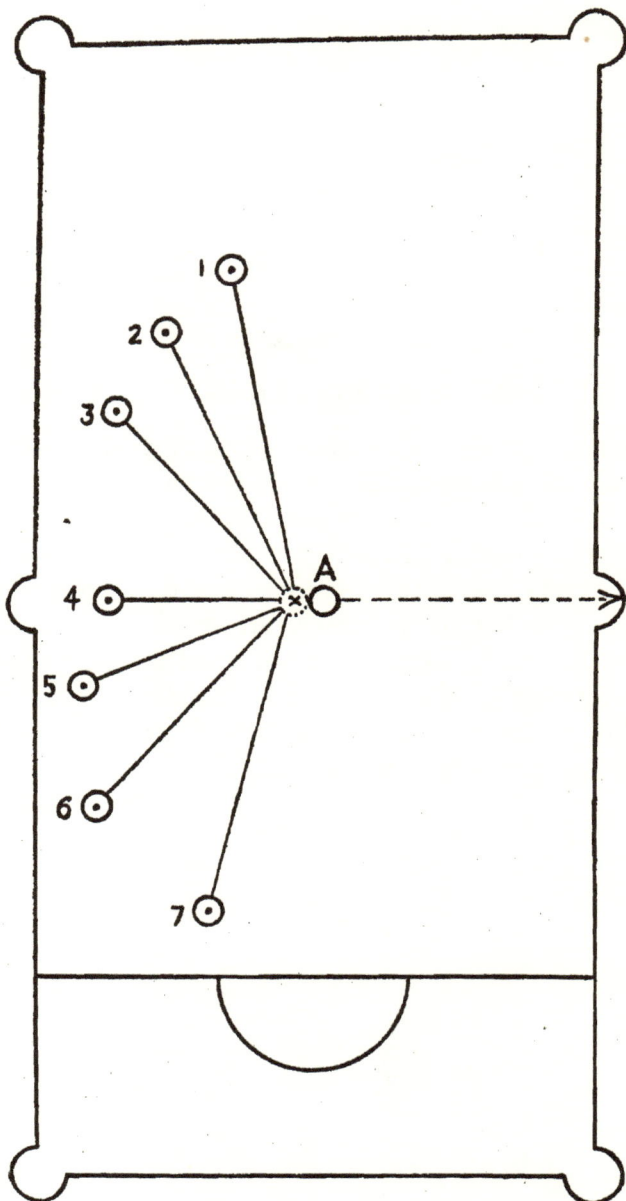

DIAGRAM 6

THE WINNING HAZARD

To pot A, which is on the blue spot, in middle pocket, Position 4 for the cue ball involves a full ball contact. The dotted circle shows position of the cue ball at moment of contact with A. The centre of the cue ball must be on the point marked with a cross, to pot A, and this applies to the shot from any of the angles shown, because the same point of A must be struck, whatever the angle of approach.

CHAPTER IV

ESSENTIAL BILLIARD SHOTS:
HALF-BALL CONTACT

TAKE another look at Diagram 5, showing the pot into middle pocket from baulk.

I advised you for cueing to practise also hitting the cue ball above centre and sending it into the pocket after the red. One ought to be able to do this with certainty, but in billiards it is rarely the right game. The ordinary sequence—and you should always be thinking of the shot to follow—is to pot the red and leave the cue ball ready for an easy half-ball loser off the red after the red has been placed on the billiards spot.

This "cross-loser" must be done properly. It is an easy shot once mastered, as are all the half-ball plain shots; but many amateurs play it carelessly and while perhaps scoring the in-off they often place the red in baulk or against a side cushion. If the red is struck about half-ball, without side, it will travel somewhere along the middle of the table and be playable again from baulk, perhaps leaving another middle pocket pot or an easy in-off.

Position for Cross-Loser

The correct position to be aimed for after potting red in middle pocket is shown in Diagram 7. With a little practice it will be found that by placing the cue ball in the D so that it is slightly out of the straight line with the red and the pocket, the red is pocketed and the cue ball travels a little up table at a tangent, remaining in the line of aim from middle pocket to billiards spot.

Played this way, the cue ball can be kept well off the cushion.

An easier way of obtaining the position for the cross-loser is to let the cue ball follow through almost straight after the red, and come off the farther shoulder of the pocket, or off the side cushion above the middle pocket very softly. Perhaps there is a little more danger of leaving the cue ball too far up the side of the table. You will soon discover which way of doing the shot suits you best. If the cue ball is allowed to go too far up the table, the position is awkward. Instead of an easy half-ball in-off the red, there is either a thin in-off, which may be difficult to judge, or a pot at an uncertain angle.

The special value of these essential shots, apart from the frequency of their occurrence, is the possibility of the easy follow-up. Hence, in practising them, your care should be for the next position quite as much as for the single shot. When we come to more difficult but less essential shots, it may be that the majority of amateurs should think less of position and concentrate on not missing the individual shot at the moment.

Top End Loser

Once you can get correct position for the cross-loser, off the billiards spot, and play the cross-loser correctly with confidence, the next of these essential half-ball shots that I show in Diagram 8 should present no difficulties.

The situation often arises where you have an easy pot red into one of the top pockets and can leave the cue ball near the pocket. When doing so, aim to leave the cue ball not only near the pocket but nearer the top cushion than the side cushion.

Should you get the cue ball an inch or two away from the pocket along the top cushion, the in-off, though no longer exactly half-ball, being a slightly wider shot, is easier than the thin in-off that results if the cue ball is a couple of inches or more along the side cushion.

When the shot is wider, the red can be hit a little more full than half-ball, and if played not too hard, some running side will help to carry the cue ball into the corner pocket. But we shall come to the use of side later. I want you to play these half-ball shots accurately first. As shown in Diagram 8, this particular in-off from one corner to the other is played at sufficient strength to send the red at least as far as the middle pocket, usually after striking the side cushion. It is then ready for another easy shot played from baulk.

Loser off Centre Spot

The stroke necessary for the shot shown in Diagram 9 is also a plain half-ball when the object ball is on the centre spot of the table. When the object ball is left somewhere near but not on centre spot, judgment must be used in placing the cue ball at the right point along the baulk line, but you should practise the shot at first as shown, until you can feel the right thickness wanted on the object ball and also the right strength to bring it round, as shown by the dotted line, to another favourable position for scoring. If the strength is sufficient there is considerable margin for error in the angle taken by the object ball. It may come back near the middle of the table, or as shown by the dotted line, between middle pocket and the D.

Diagram 10 shows a valuable and common plain ball in-off to middle pocket, where the position of the object ball is not fixed. Here again there is considerable margin allowable in the direction taken by the object ball, care being taken chiefly to keep it near the middle of the table and to bring it back well away from top cushion at least, if not as far as where it was, which is preferable.

Positional Cannons

Cannons count two in billiards, but with amateurs they so often also mean the end of the break because of a bad position left after the cannon.

If you have grasped these elements of cueing and aiming, you will find that it is often as easy to play a cannon to leave a good position after as to play it and leave nothing to follow.

In Diagram 11 is a cannon position. The cannon should be played with the idea of sending the object ball up the table towards the destination of the cue ball, as this will leave all the balls more or less together at the top of the table. The exact half-ball contact may not always be feasible in doing this, but once you have mastered the half-ball plain stroke you will have little difficulty in varying the thickness of the contact to get the most convenient position. Sometimes, if the object ball is already above the middle pocket, it can be played 'rather thinner to get position, especially if it is near the side cushion, because then with less force of impact it will come off the cushion sufficiently for your purpose. This is another cannon of the same type, known as the "drop cannon," getting all the balls at the top end of the table. The principle of this cannon is that the object ball must be struck with the thickness and strength required to leave it at the top end of the table near the others. If you examine the position shown in Diagram 11 you will see that the cannon could be scored by a fairly fast stroke, but striking the object ball too thin to send it to the top end.

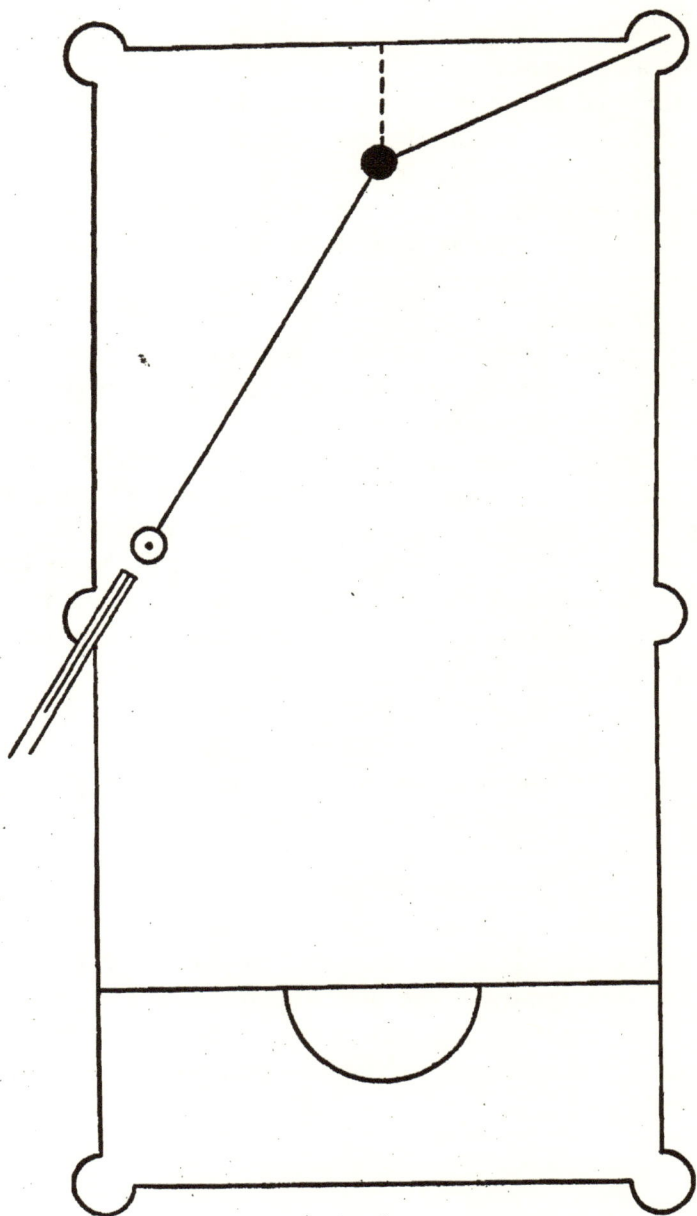

DIAGRAM 7

PLAIN HALF-BALL SHOTS, NO. 1

The losing hazard off red on its spot, from middle pocket. If correctly struck, the red ball should travel down the middle of the table after rebounding from top cushion. See page 24.

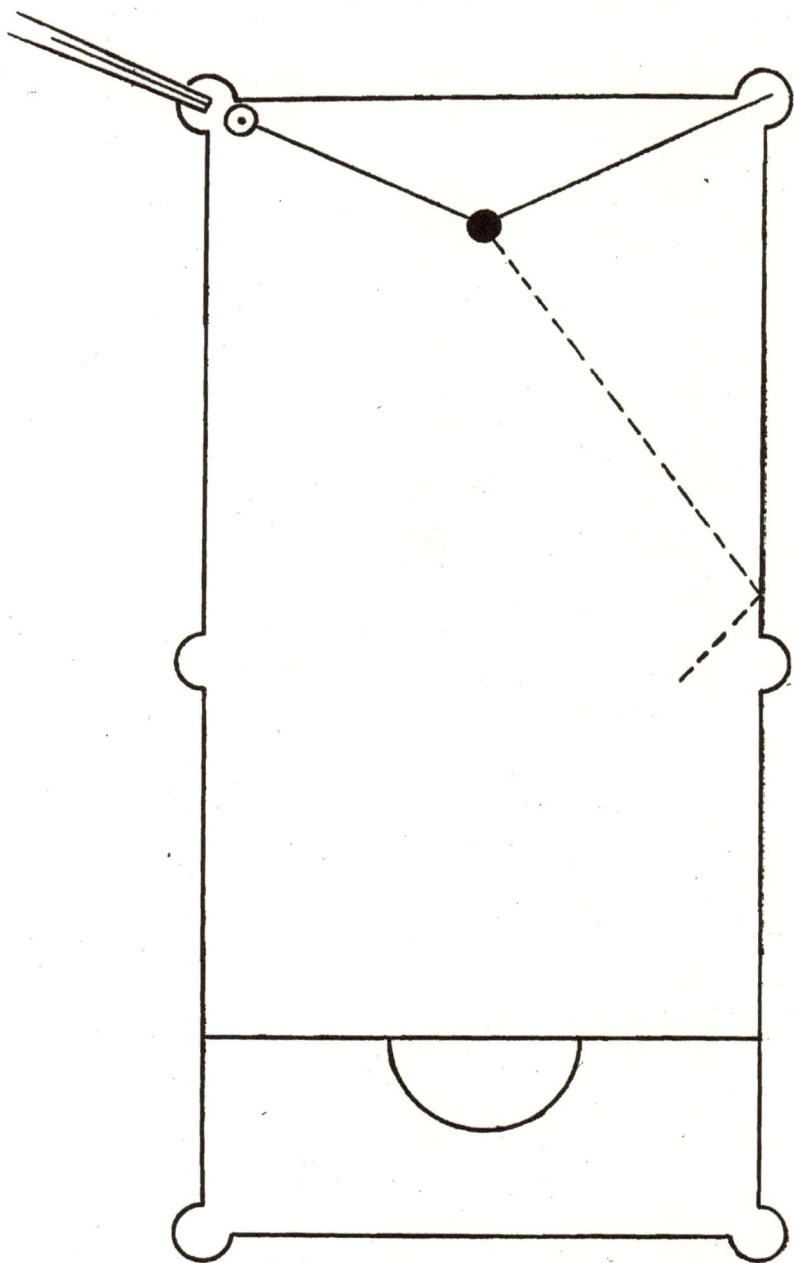

DIAGRAM 8

PLAIN HALF-BALL SHOTS, NO. 2

The losing hazard off the red on its spot, into top pocket, when the cue ball is near top cushion and opposite top pocket. It is played at sufficient strength to send the red ball off side cushion and a little below the middle pocket, ready for the next shot with the cue ball in hand. See page 25.

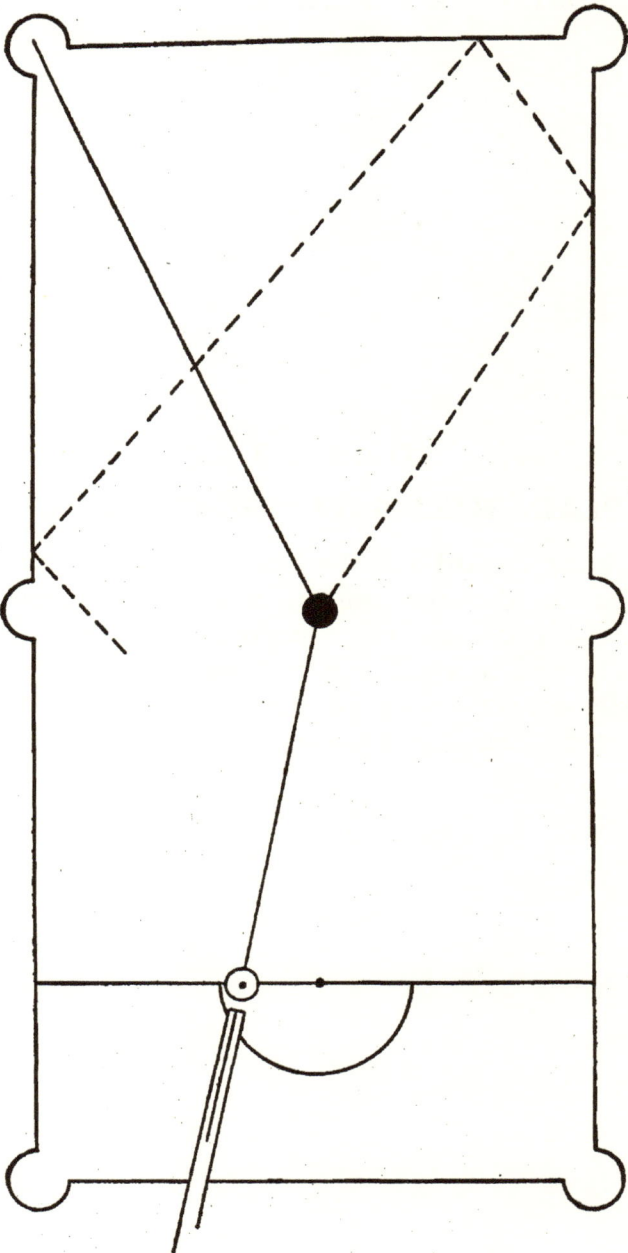

DIAGRAM 9

PLAIN HALF-BALL SHOTS, NO. 3

The object ball is on the centre spot (on blue spot in snooker); the cue ball is in hand. A half-ball contact on the object ball is made for a losing hazard into top pocket, driving the object ball round as shown by dotted lines, and leaving it where it may be played again, for an in-off, or a pot into middle pocket. See page 26.

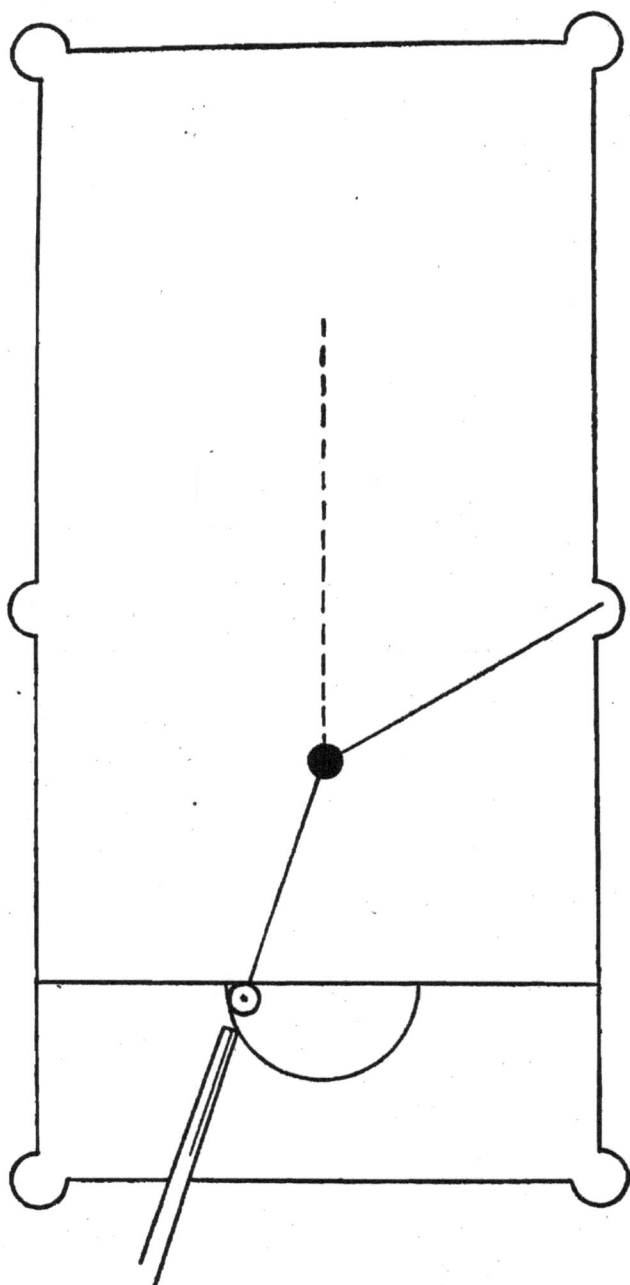

DIAGRAM 10

PLAIN HALF-BALL SHOTS, NO. 4

Unlike the three previous shots (Diagrams 5 to 7), this middle pocket loser, although a common one, is not a shot with fixed position for the object ball. As the cue ball is in hand, judgment must be used as to where to place it for the plain half-ball stroke, which should keep the object ball roughly in the middle of the table and bring it off top cushion to somewhere near where it was.

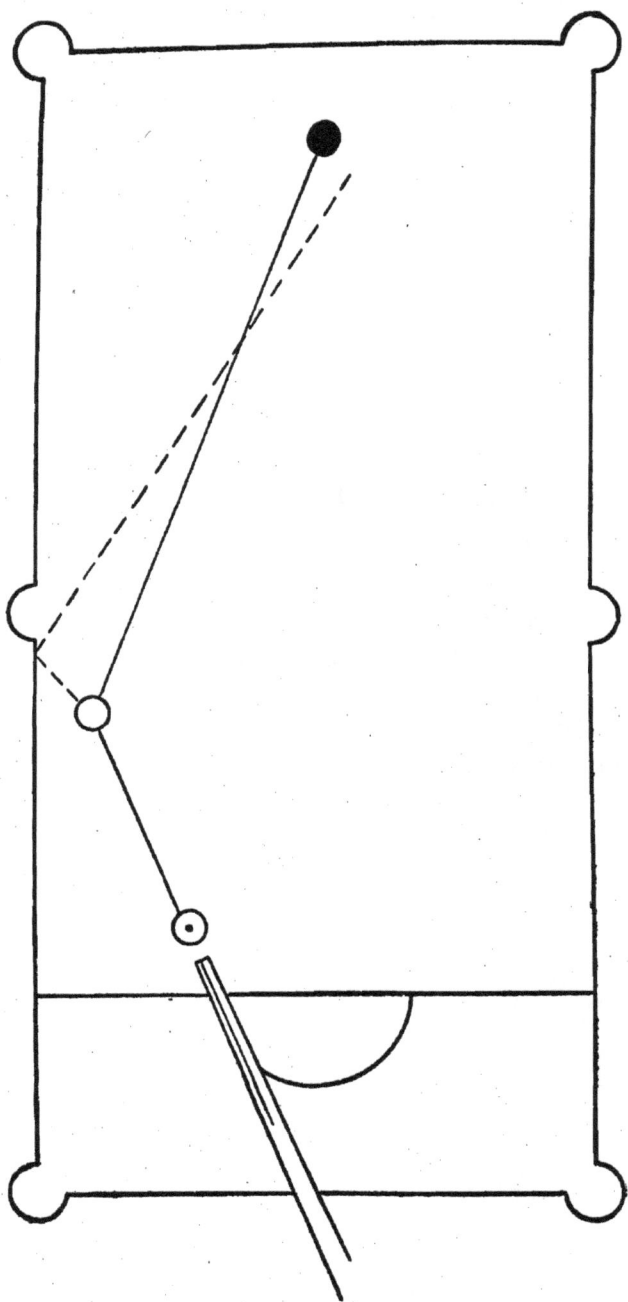

36

DIAGRAM 11

PLAIN HALF-BALL SHOTS, NO. 5

The half-ball stroke without side should be made good use of for cannons like this one, to gather the balls together up the table. The good player often starts a "break" with such a shot. Sometimes the "drop cannon," as such a positional shot is called, cannot be made with a half-ball contact, as the angle would not bring the balls together. See end of Chapter III and Diagram 24 on page 76.

CHAPTER V

SCREW OR DRAG

COUNTLESS shots in both snooker and billiards depend upon imparting to the cue ball a rotation additional to the ordinary forward rotation that results from striking it centrally for a plain stroke.

You have seen the result of striking the cue ball high in practising the "six shot" into middle pocket from baulk, making the white follow the red into the pocket. This had to be done without any lateral deviation of the white; in other words the white was struck above centre but not to one side.

The Stroke

Screw is the opposite of "top." Instead of making the cue ball follow through, it brings it back. The stroke is very low, care being taken not to point the cue downwards much more than usual, but to lower the whole cue when making it. The backward rotation imparted to the cue ball takes full effect after it has struck the object ball and lost its forward momentum.

Many players try to get screw by hitting hard, but it is not the strength of the stroke that achieves the result. Mere strength only hurls the ball forward faster; though it may send it off the object ball more squarely, it does not help to bring it back. The backward roll is achieved by precision in the stroke, the cue being allowed to follow on in the direction of the stroke as usual, the only difference being that it is on a lower level. Only if the balls are very near each other is there any need for a "jab," the cue being withdrawn very sharply after striking cue ball.

38

" Stun "

In snooker the "stun" shot is extremely useful. This is not quite a screw. The cue ball stops dead after striking the object ball because it has enough backward rotation just to cancel the forward momentum, but not enough to make it roll backwards.

In Diagram 13 is a useful exercise recommended by my uncle, Walter, for the screw stroke. Once you have mastered the screw, the stun is quite simple. This exercise is not easy except to a very good cueist, so do not be discouraged at unsatisfactory results when trying it, but try also one or two common and useful billiard shots such as the in-offs and the cannon shown in Diagram 14, and the snooker shots in Diagram 15. Then examine the following.

DIAGRAM 12

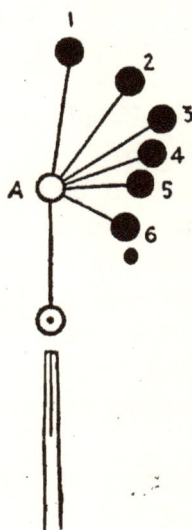

Direction after Contact

In the above diagram I am trying to illustrate the

important difference in the direction taken by the cue ball after contact with the object ball according to the kind of stroke made.

As slight variations in the strokes as played are inevitable, the diagram is only approximate, though it distinguishes clearly between the various kinds of stroke required for the cannon. Snooker players should remember that this control of direction after contact is just as important in snooker as it is in billiards. Instead of a cannon, the object may be a snooker, the avoidance of an in-off, or a follow-up shot.

Taking the balls numbered 1 to 6 as each being the third ball which the cue ball has to reach after striking the object ball (Marked A), we have various amounts of forward or backward rotation of the cue ball.

The follow-through cannon, No. 1, can be done only by putting top on the cue ball. No. 2 is a half follow-through, the object ball being struck between half-ball and three-quarter ball with plenty of top on the cue ball.

No. 3 is the ordinary half-ball stroke, without top or bottom, at medium strength.

No. 4 is interesting. It can be done with a plain ball stroke played harder than usual, called a "forcer," or it can be done by striking the cue ball a little lower than centre at medium strength. No. 5 requires about three-quarter ball contact as well as screw, and No. 6 calls for an almost full ball contact and still more screw. Remember that the more screw wanted, the fuller the contact must be.

For these strokes I assume that the cue ball is not too far away from the object ball, say about 18 inches or less, because the farther the cue ball has to travel before striking the object ball the harder it is to make it retain screw or "drag," and I want you to tackle these strokes under favourable conditions before trying difficult cueing feats.

The right angle screw, No. 5, is especially important for practice, once you can do the screw straight back shown in Diagram 13, because it is the next easiest to measure for direction. It is often very useful in snooker for opening up the reds when potting a colour. Sometimes side is necessary also, for this; but one thing at a time.

In billiards the screw cannon is a commonly useful positional shot for gathering the balls together instead of spreading them worse than they are.

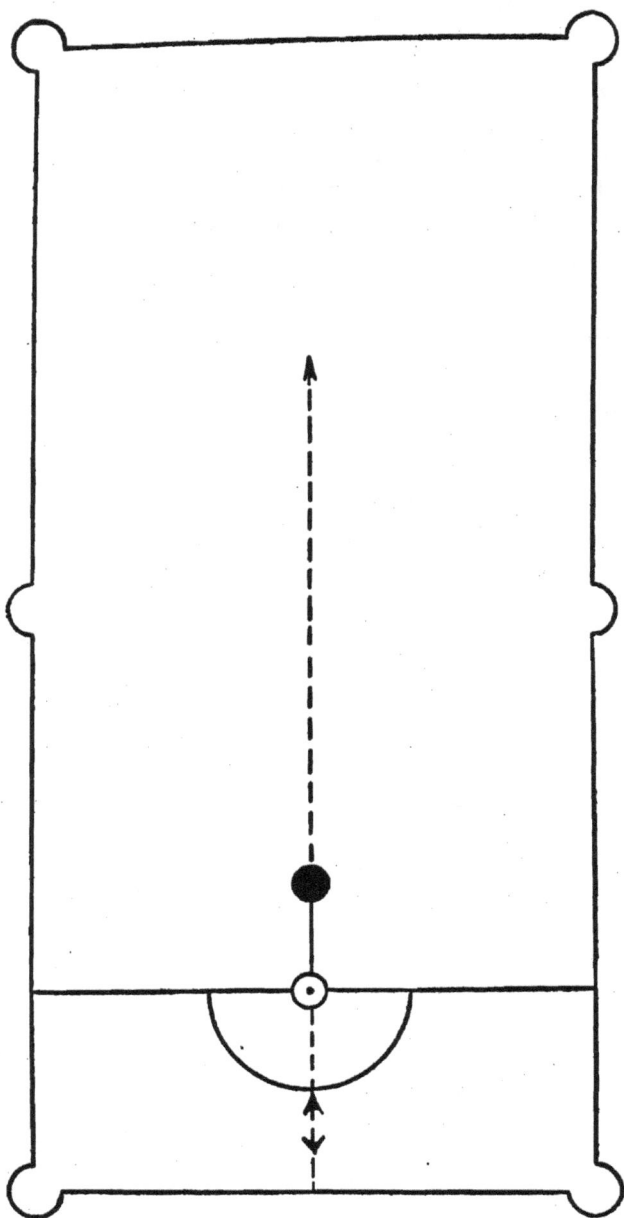

DIAGRAM 13

SCREW BACK

This is not an easy exercise. Walter Lindrum recommends that you should play on the object ball, from the brown spot of the D, and screw straight back to bottom cushion and make the cue ball rebound to the brown spot again. Even if you cannot do this, you should be able to screw straight back to the cushion, and send the object ball fairly straight up the middle of the table and back. It will assist firmness in the stroke to replace the ordinary bridge by looping forefinger round the cue.

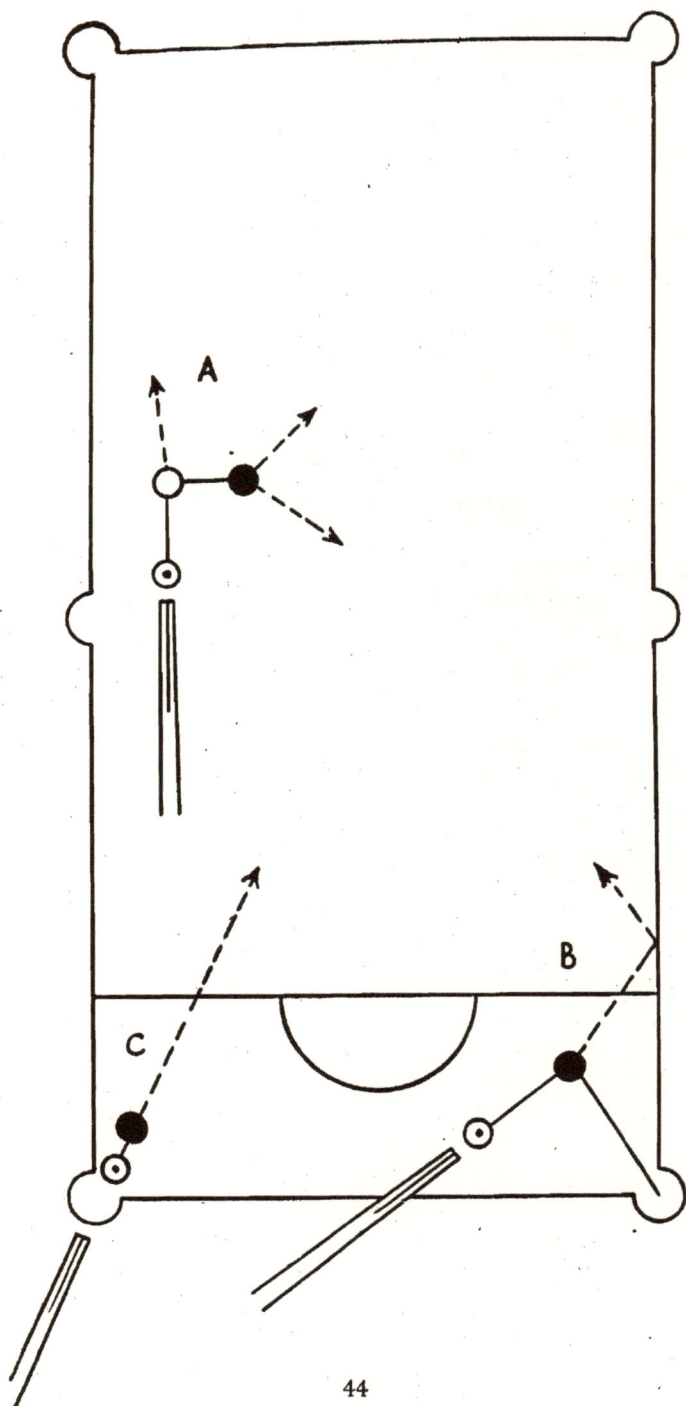

DIAGRAM 14

BILLIARD SCREW SHOTS

A is a right-angled cannon (not necessarily the right shot to do) which need not be played hard at closer quarters. In proper play you would try to strike the red on the near side to keep it up the table, or you might, with less screw, try to strike it a little behind, to send it towards middle pocket. The screw in-off B and C would probably leave good positions, the object ball being sent up the table at the right strength. Avoid unnecessary force in the stroke. When these in-offs occur at the top end it is usually desirable to play them hard enough to bring the object ball back after sending it down the table.

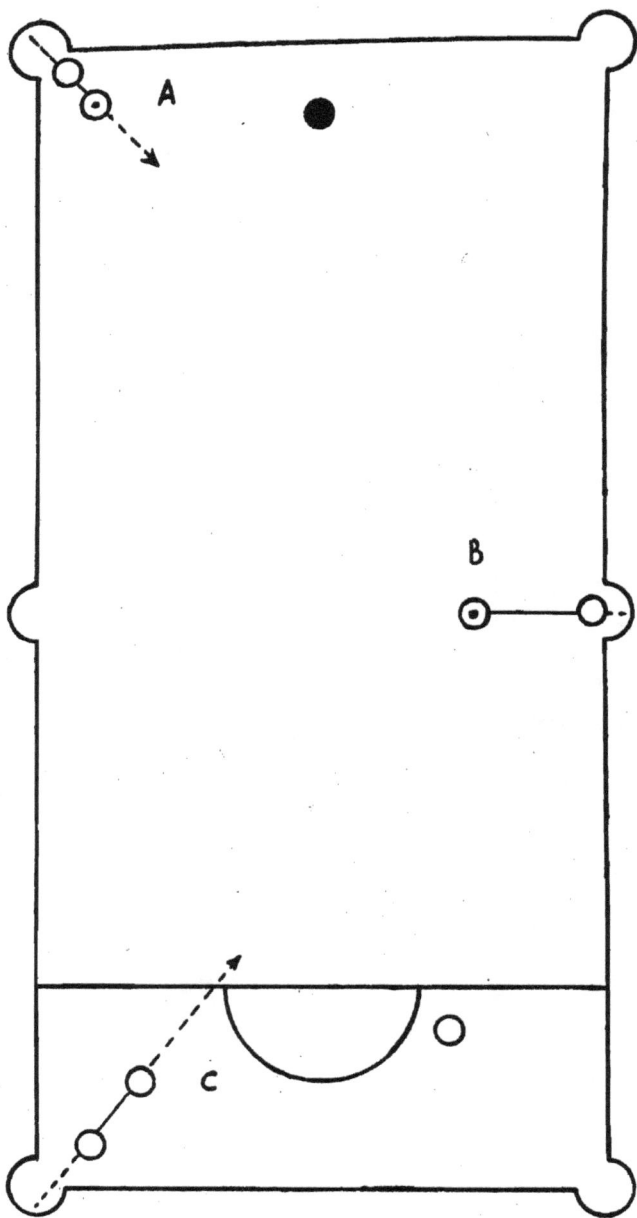

DIAGRAM 15

SNOOKER SCREW AND STUN SHOTS

Simple examples like the above are continually cropping up in snooker.

A. After potting ball in top left hand pocket bring cue ball back a little for straight pot on black.

B. Many an expensive "in-off" is due to the player not stunning the cue-ball (see page 39). In this position it is very easy to stop the cue ball dead where it strikes the object ball.

C. This is similar to A, except that the next ball on is not on a recognized spot. Without screwing back after the pot into the bottom left-hand pocket, an awkward cut would be left, with a possible "in-off" in middle pocket after it. Played as shown, a fairly straight pot follows into opposite corner pocket.

CHAPTER VI

SIDE AND HOW TO USE IT

SIDE is the lateral rotation of the cue ball in addition to its forward rotation, and is obtained by striking the ball to one side. This may be done in conjunction with either screw or top, a combination very useful for some of the more exact positional strokes in snooker and billiards. But the generally useful stroke with side avoids this complication. Moreover maximum effect of side can only be obtained when the ball is struck on the side not too low. If you think of a clock face, this means at about between 8.30 and 9, and 3 and 3.30, near the edge, but not too near, or the cue will tend to slip past the ball and push it sideways.

Swerve

This tendency can be exploited to "swerve" the ball, by pointing the cue downwards and striking the ball rather low on the side required, that is about 7.30 or 4.30 on our imaginary clock face. The swerve shot is shown in Diagram 33 and is useful in snooker. It is the first step towards the masse stroke. Now let us get back to our subject.

" Check " and " Running "

The terms "check side" and "running side" are constantly used, but are not always understood. If you say right-hand or left-hand side, it means nothing until you see the actual shot to which it refers. In the following diagram suppose that A and B shots are both played with right-hand side. That is to say, the cue ball is struck on the right. But in A this right-hand side is correctly called "running" side, while in B it is "check."

DIAGRAM 16

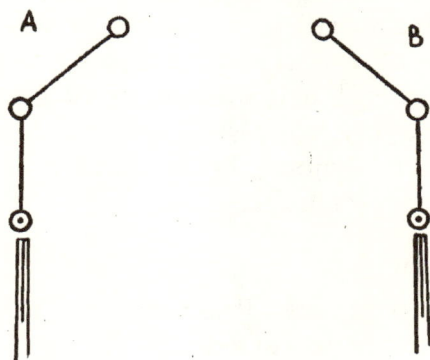

What is the difference between "running" and "check" side then? The effect is described in the terms used. Running side makes the cue ball run more after contact with either the object ball or a cushion, while check side tends to slow it down.

The reason for this is explained by the definition of "running side" and "check side." Running side is the side put on the cue ball that corresponds to the direction after contact, while check side is the side put on the cue ball opposite to the direction after contact.

Look at the above diagram. You will see that in A the right-hand side is running side because the cue ball travels to the right after striking the object ball, while in B the right-hand side is check because it is against the direction of the cue ball, which travels to the left.

This side rotation of the cue ball is immensely important in both billiards and snooker, and you should study it carefully. A whole book could be written on it, and some of the questions involved by it are still matters of controversy. One of these, the question of "transmitted" side, I propose to try and clear up, as amateurs are constantly arguing about it, although for practical purposes the amateur may ignore it. As he will not do so without being convinced, having heard such contradictory opinions, it seems worth some attention. Before I give you an outline of the scientific theory and the facts about this, however, I will show some of the commonest uses of side in playing, that is, side on the cue ball. For the moment let us ignore the possibility of side being imparted to the object ball.

Shots with Side

Diagrams 17 to 19 are all devoted to important shots that depend upon the use of side.

In playing them remember that the strength of the stroke is an important factor.

The in-off shown in Diagram 17(c) is much easier than it looks, but the cannon shown in Diagram 18(A) is more difficult because a little top as well as side is wanted and the stroke must be very true. Moreover, if played straight *down* the table, against the nap, it wants check instead of running side. But both shots depend on the behaviour of the cue ball with side.

With running side the cue ball does not travel straight after contact, but swerves more or less, according to strength and fullness of contact, as shown by the line leading to the pocket for the in-off in Diagram 17.

The follow-through cannon with the "impossible" position (as many amateurs would describe it) in 18(A) also depends on this outward curve of the cue ball after striking the object ball.

Check side makes the cue ball travel much straighter after contact, because the rotation is opposed to the new direction set up by the contact with the other ball. Hence for certain thin in-offs and cannons it is useful because it helps to prevent the cue ball travelling outwards, and it is often helpful in snooker to prevent an in-off, as in Diagram 18(c).

Side off a Cushion

Remember also that if you want the side to take effect off a cushion the shot must not be played hard. A hard stroke will cause the cue ball to spring off the cushion at an incalculable angle. In getting out of a snooker by a cushion shot this is important if the necessary angle depends on the use of side, as shown in Diagram 18(b).

One other warning about the effect of side. If you play a fairly slow shot with a lot of side, going up the table with the nap, the ball will run off slightly towards the direction of the side, while playing the same shot against the nap, down table, it will run off in the direction opposite to that of the side. This is why the thin loser into the bottom pocket, and the follow-through, shown in Diagram 22, call for running side. In each case here running side is opposite to that of the cushion, which you want the cue ball to hug.

Now for the notorious "transmitted side."

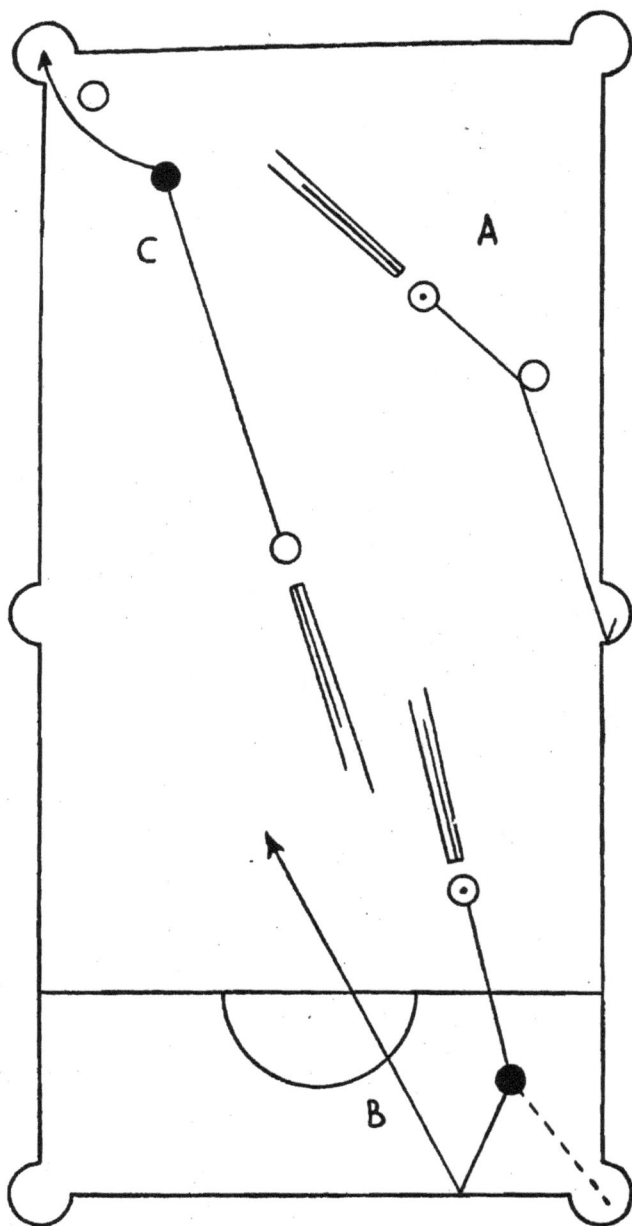

DIAGRAM 17

SHOTS WITH SIDE

A. The rather thin in-off is aided by left-hand (check side) because, the pocket being half covered by the nearer shoulder, aim is made on the farther shoulder. The check side on the cue-ball turns it into the pocket after striking the inside of the shoulder, whereas running side would bring it away.

B. If it is desired to come well up the table after a pot in this kind of position, running side (here, right) will make all the difference, and save the need for force.

C. This in-off would be impossible without running (left) side, which causes the cue ball to curl outwards after contact with object ball, so avoiding the ball that half covers the pocket.

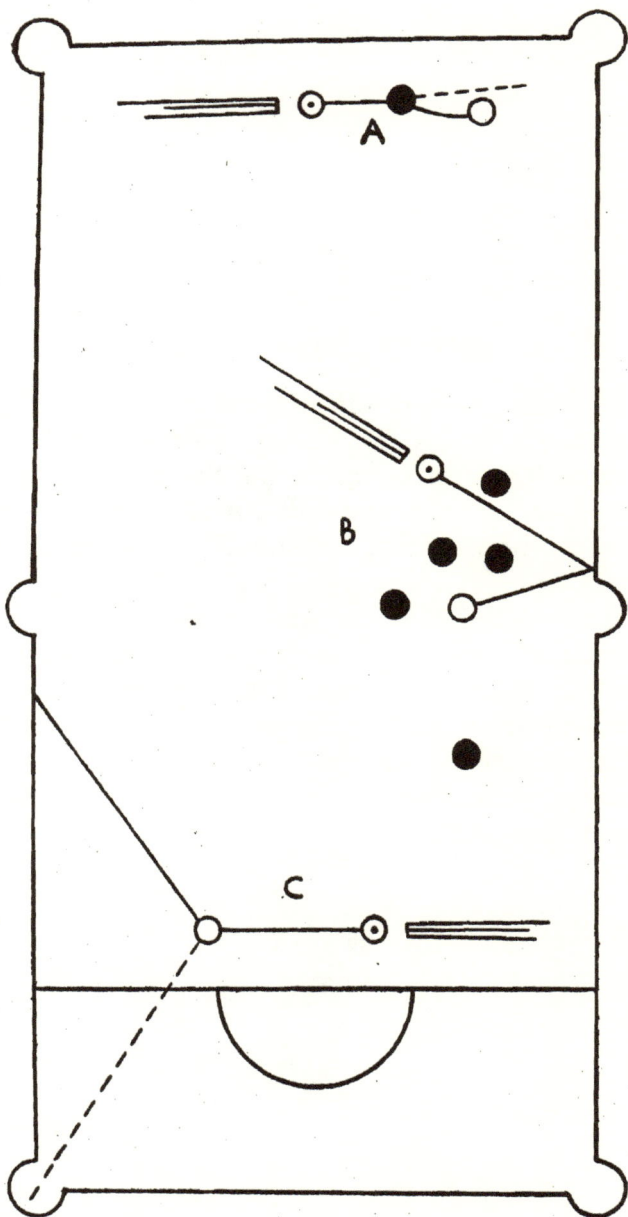

DIAGRAM 18

MORE SHOTS WITH SIDE

A. The balls are too nearly in a straight line for a clear follow-through cannon, yet if running (right) side be put on cue ball, the red being played to just clear the other white, the cue ball will swerve slightly to the right after contact and make the cannon. In snooker the same principle can be useful if you want to snooker behind the third ball. But this shot dead against the nap will need the opposite side on cue ball.

B. Getting out of a snooker by playing off the cushion. Owing to obstacles, the ordinary angle is impossible, but if the cushion is struck as indicated with check (left) side, the cue ball will come off cushion at a narrower angle to reach the object ball.

C. In snooker the player often fears an in-off while potting. Here he might fear to run into middle pocket. The cue ball will travel straighter towards cushion with check (left) side. It also reduces the speed of the cue ball after contact.

CHAPTER VII

TRANSMITTED SIDE

Some leading professionals, including my uncle, Walter, and Willie Smith, have declared that the proof of the pudding is in the eating, and quite right, too. They declare that they can make use of the effect of side being transmitted to the object ball. Others, supported by mathematical theory, say that it is impossible to impart rotation to the object ball by putting side on the cue ball, and that, anyhow, why is it so difficult to observe if it constantly happens?

Both sides are right in a sense.

But both sides tend to exaggerate the truth.

It is true that transmitted side is extremely difficult to observe, that is with the eye watching the object ball. Yet some very delicate shots, especially close cannons, are achieved because the object ball has gained a very slight amount of side from the cue ball.

But those who say that the object ball is affected by the side of the cue ball, though without having any rotation that could be called "side," are also largely justified.

Noticeable deviations in the course of the object ball due to side on the cue ball are, I feel sure, not due to transmitted side at all, but to a deflection of the course of the object ball, as declared by Stanley Newman in his book on snooker. What he does not say, however, and what supplies an answer to the overstatements of the other camp, is this.

Deflection of Object-Ball

The object ball is often noticeably deflected when side

is put on the cue ball because the shot is done by striking the object ball at a slightly different point than it would be with either no side or the opposite side to that used. I can show this by an illustration given in Walter's book to prove the effect of transmitted side. This is in Diagram 19.

· It seems obvious, once you realize that there are two sorts of effect produced on the object ball by side on the cue ball that the big difference between A and B in the diagram is not due to transmitted side but to the red ball being struck differently.

I have just been explaining that with running side the cue ball curls outwards after contact, whereas with check side it travels straighter. If you look at the two in-offs in the diagram, you will see that A (running side) can be done with a slightly thicker contact on the red than B (check side).

The best way is to try it for yourself.

Now, the effect of striking the red thinner would be to send it farther across the table, while striking it fuller would keep it nearer to the same side of the table.

As a matter of fact the principle is always being applied in playing losing hazards and keeping the object ball in a favourable position for the next shot. Which shows that masters of the practical side of the game like Willie Smith and Walter Lindrum are fallible on theory. Convinced that transmitted side occurs in some shots, they (and others) attribute the more obvious deflections of the object ball to the same cause, whereas a simpler explanation confronts us.

Theory and Fact

Why is transmitted side difficult to observe?

Because it is very, very slight, and can affect only the most delicate close play.

Why is it so slight?

Mathematically, it is impossible. If you had two perfect balls, with perfectly clean and frictionless surfaces that offered only the tiny point of contact that is made between two spheres, however fast sphere A was rotating when it struck sphere B, the contact would be equivalent to a tap on one point, imparting merely a forward motion to B. There is no arguing about this. Any mathematician would confirm it.

But in practice balls are not perfectly clean. Sometimes anything but! Neither is the table. The use of chalk alone would prevent it, even in a professional match where new balls and new cloth were used. This means that the surface of the balls offers a slight amount of rub or friction on contact, and if ball A is rotating in a certain way on its axis as well as forward, it would at the moment of contact rub the surface of B and set up a slight tendency to rotate in the opposite lateral direction. The fact that this can happen, apart from the weighty testimony of first-class players who know what they are doing, has been proved by a mechanical iron contrivance for making true strokes much more powerful than a man wielding a cue can make.

Having stated, and partly explained away, the views of Walter Lindrum and Willie Smith, I will conclude by referring to the chief spokesman on the other side, no less a cueman than the late Tom Newman, the eminent brother of Stanley Newman, whom I have referred to already.

He agreed that the usually observed effect on the object ball is due to the stroke being played with a slight difference when side is used on the cue ball, but because this is miscalled "transmitted side" by great players who are weak on theory, Tom assumed that *no* transmitted side can have "the smallest influence on the game in being."

Well, I should prefer to accept Walter Lindrum's testimony that it does matter to him for the most delicate shots, particularly cushion-cannons and so on, although he was quite wrong about the more obvious deflection of · the object ball. Tom Newman, however, followed up his broadside with the interesting statement in the *Billiards and Snooker* magazine, edited by Mr. W. G. Clifford: · "I can vouch that I have never played a stroke in my life in which I made the least allowance for the transmission of side unless the object ball is right against the cushion." That final "unless," of course, meets Walter half-way, and the amateur who has now a view of both sides of the question may well leave the discussion as to how many kinds of delicate shots require transmitted side to leading professionals. Tom Newman's attitude, without his "unless," was the practical, common-sense one for any amateur, however good, because transmitted side will never be a big enough factor to affect his play to any noticeable degree.

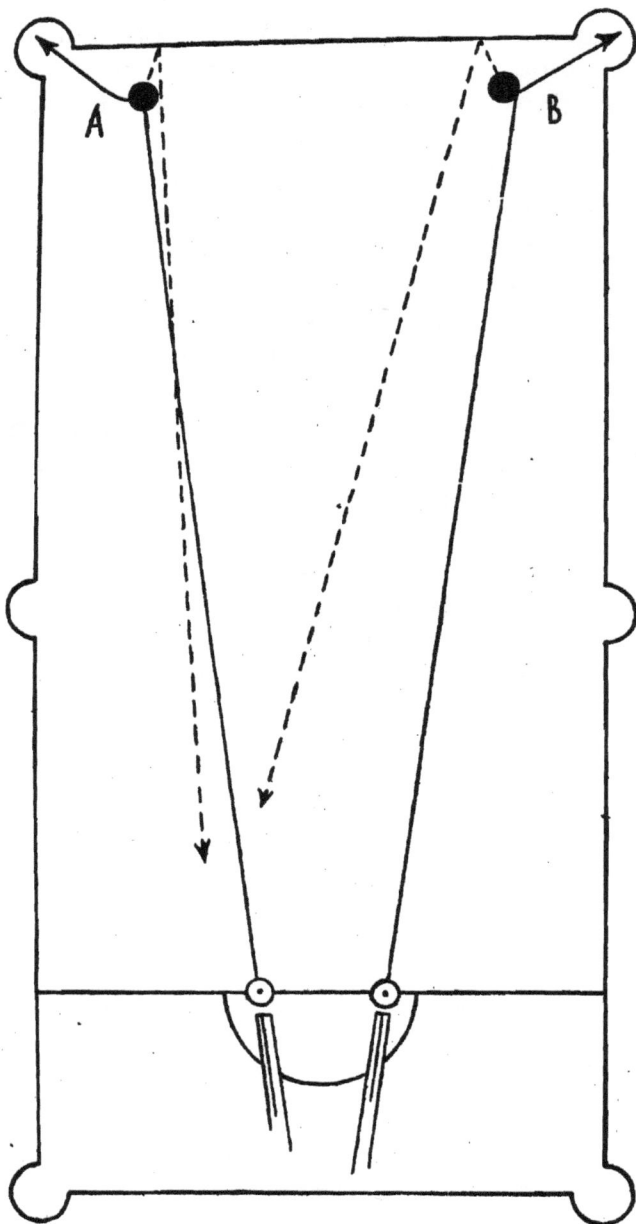

Diagram 19

IS THIS TRANSMITTED SIDE ?

As explained on page 57, the above is similar to a diagram given by Walter Lindrum to show the effects of transmitted side. A is played with running (left) side, while B is played with check (left) side. Walter claims that the red in A comes off the top cushion straighter and keeps to the same side of the table because it has acquired side from the cue ball. Similarly in B, having the opposite rotation it comes off at a wider angle and travels farther across the table.

I do not believe that the tiny possible amount of transmitted side could achieve these obvious results. My explanation is much simpler, and applies to many common positional shots.

CHAPTER VIII

EFFECT OF THE NAP

You cannot expect to build up breaks in either snooker or billiards without making proper use of the nap. The cloth has a nap on it which lies towards the top cushion, as may be seen if the finger is rubbed gently towards the bottom cushion. It will leave a mark that is caused by the nap being lifted. Hence playing up the table is playing with the nap, and playing down the table towards baulk is against the nap.

Pot Due to Nap

The simplest illustration of the effect upon play of the nap is the very slow pot into middle pocket at an "impossible" angle, the pocket being covered by the nearer shoulder. This is A in Diagram 20. If you try the same shot from below the pocket, that is with the nap, you will find that it cannot be done. But when the object ball is running against the nap towards the farther bump of the pocket, the nap will curl it into the pocket. The shot must be done very slowly, so that the object ball has hardly any more momentum by the time it reaches the space opposite the pocket.

B in Diagram 20 is another, more common, winning hazard, the cut being favourable to the slow speed required. The aim is to cut the object ball as if you wanted it to reach the farther shoulder of the middle pocket. Such a pot in snooker is frequently valuable as a positional shot, coming back perhaps for the black or pink.

Many a double into the middle pocket can be done slowly on the same principle when a faster shot is undesirable, the aim being to double the object ball slightly beyond the jaw of pocket, letting the nap coax it off its course to the pocket.

When Side is Reversed

Diagrams 21 to 23 explain the effect of nap upon play in various useful billiard shots, and I need not add much to my previous remarks and the captions with the Diagrams. I do not think that the curious effect of the nap in reversing the side that is wanted, as shown in Diagrams 21 and 22, has ever been satisfactorily explained, but a practical knowledge of it is essential to the good player. Another shot affected is A in Diagram 18.

Any player who has assimilated the experience covered in these chapters so far should be able to play all the most useful shots necessary for a good game of billiards or snooker, though of course there are a great number of various shots, and all I can do is to draw your attention to as many as possible which are likely to be most valuable.

By treating billiards and snooker together so far I hope I have emphasized the essential principles upon which both depend. My own play, I feel, has always relied upon as much similarity of style in both games as possible.

The real difference, apart from the rules and tactics of each game, is that in snooker a comparatively smaller number of shots predominate, while in billiards at least half of the commonest shots do not come into snooker, and the variations of the basic shots are far more numerous and subtle. Nevertheless a knowledge of purely billiard shots, like cannons and losing hazards, is undoubtedly a help to good snooker. The man who plays billiards as well as snooker, other things being equal, will always beat the man who plays only snooker, especially in positional strokes.

I propose now to examine some interesting differences between the two games.

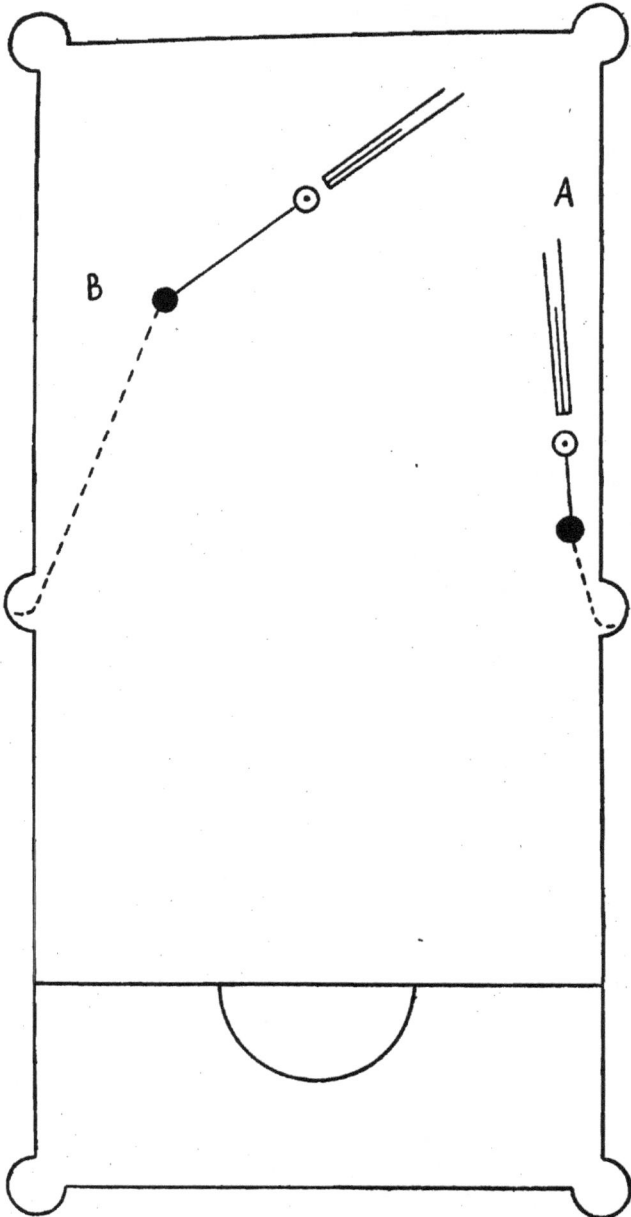

Diagram 20

WHEN THE NAP HELPS POTTING

These are typical of the slow winning hazards which depend upon the resistance of the nap, which always pushes a slow ball towards the top end. Hence a ball travelling slightly across the table against the nap is pushed off its course, a little more across. An "impossible" angle like that in A wants only a very soft stroke to let the nap push the ball into the pocket. In both A and B you aim at the further "bump." Doubles or "trebles" played slowly can also be done with the help of the nap, the ball being slightly diverted in the direction of the top end.

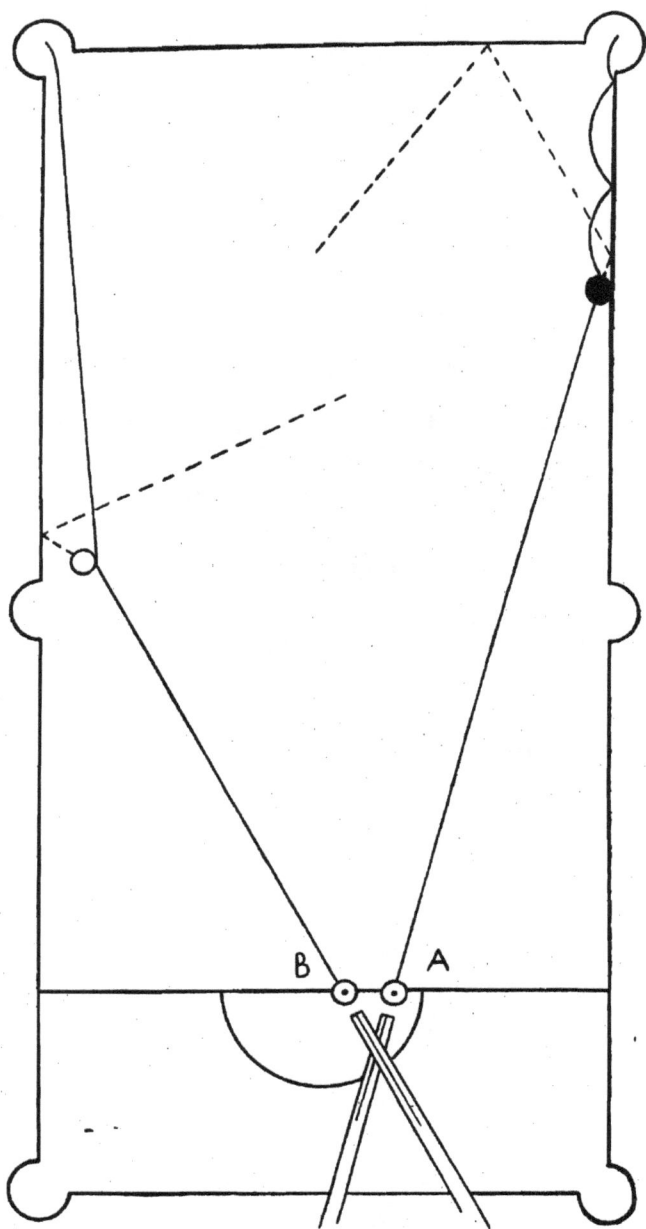

DIAGRAM 21

USE OF SIDE WITH NAP

Playing up the table, with the nap, check side causes the cue ball to hug the cushion, as in A, which is a follow-through red into top right-hand pocket. Plenty of right-hand side and strike red full. The red is driven across to top of table.

B shows the fairly thin long jenny into top left-hand pocket with plenty of check (left-hand) side on cue ball. The side will make the cue ball curl in off the further shoulder of the pocket, or if the ball reaches the side cushion first, it will prevent the ball coming away. See next diagram.

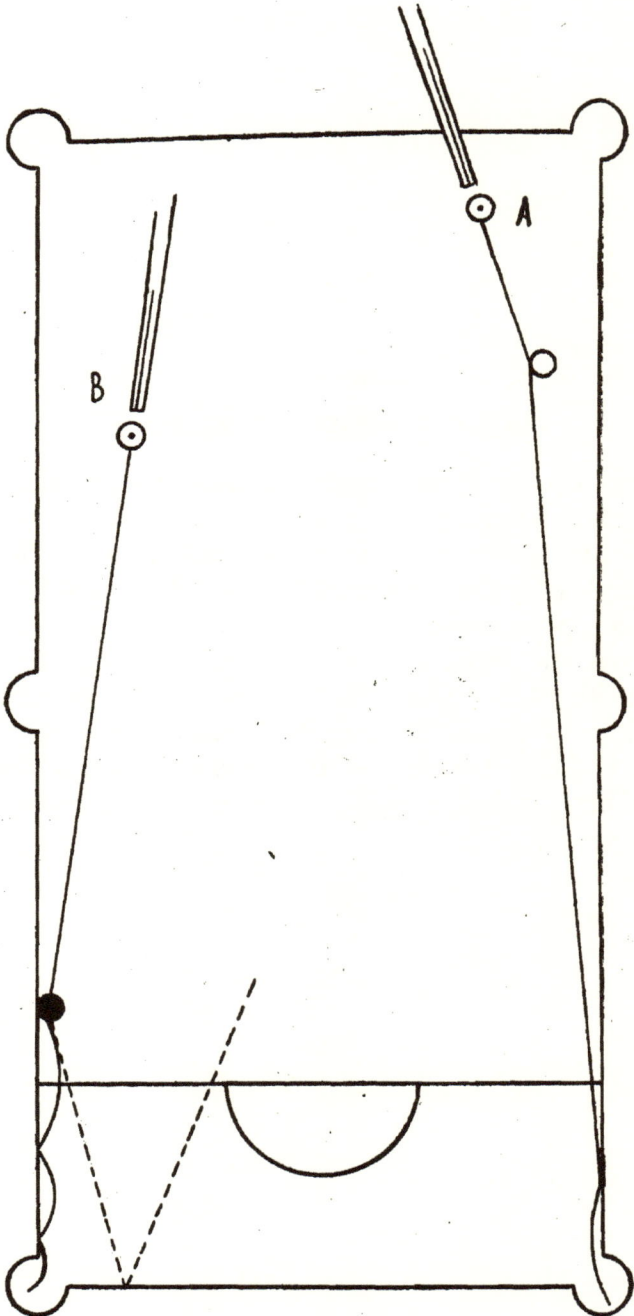

DIAGRAM 22

PLAYING AGAINST THE NAP, WITH SIDE

Instead of check side, that is used playing with the nap to keep ball against cushion (see previous diagram) the thin loser above A and the follow-through to pocket B must be played with running side. In A this is right-hand side, in B left-hand side. See page 63.

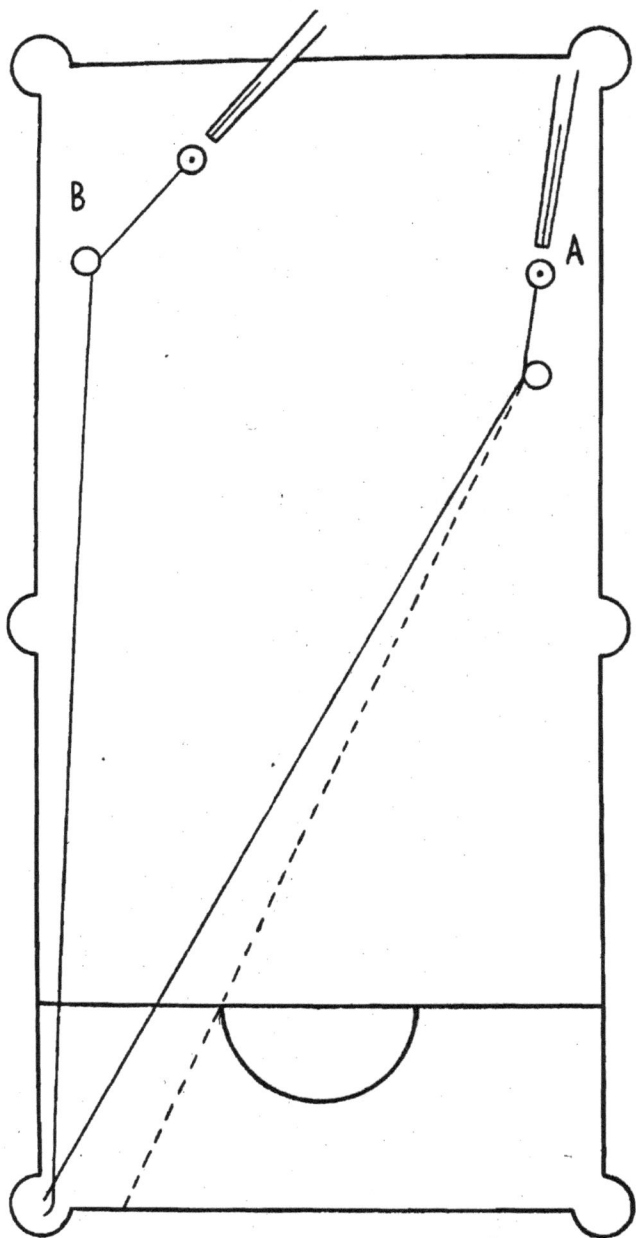

DIAGRAM 23

AGAINST THE NAP WITHOUT SIDE

The thin loser, as shown in A, is a very useful shot. It is played slowly, without side, aiming not at the pocket but a few inches along the bottom cushion, according to distance and speed, because the nap will send the ball towards the right. Dotted line shows roughly direction of the aim, if stroke is slow.

B is a contrast to the thin loser with running side shown in previous diagram. As the shot is square enough to be played with sufficient speed to ignore the nap, *check* side (right-hand here) is used, so that the farther shoulder of the pocket can be safely struck, the side carrying the ball in.

CHAPTER IX

POSITIONS IN BOTH GAMES

Many amateurs make avoidable mistakes in either billiards or snooker by introducing shots that do not belong to the game they are playing.

Old billiard players who only recently took up snooker are often bad at potting, although good at safety play, because they so often ignore a pot when it is on in a game of billiards. Actually they may play their winning hazards in a game of billiards much better than in snooker, where these are essential to victory. The best cure for this is a little practice at potting into all the pockets at various angles. Such two-ball practice will weaken the mental habit of the three-ball game so essential to billiards. Once confidence in potting has been obtained, the billiard player will find that his billiards has actually improved in the end.

Cannon or Pot

Look at Diagram 24. It shows a lovely billiard position, with the white played from hand and placed ready for the drop cannon that will gather the balls nicely near the top cushion.

Confronted with such a situation in snooker, many a billiard player will prefer a safety shot to the winning hazard which should be attempted, because he has no confidence in himself.

Actually the proper shot in snooker is to place the cue ball in hand farther along the D, as shown in Diagram 25, so that it is a fairly straight pot into top left pocket. The stroke should be made with a little drag on the cue ball to leave an easy pot into the opposite pocket of the ball on the billiard (black) spot.

Avoiding Easy Pot

In Diagram 26 I show what may be regarded as an extreme example of avoiding an easy winning hazard when playing billiards. In snooker one would not hesitate to pot the ball, putting some right (check) side and top on the cue ball to come away from bottom cushion afterwards to cut the other ball into the top left pocket.

But in billiards, if I had this position, I should not dream of potting the red in the bottom pocket, because it might be extremely difficult to do the losing hazard next off the white into the top pocket, and a cannon the length of the table with the red spotted would probably be the end of that break.

No, avoiding the easy pot here is not extreme, because the cannon that I show is much easier than it looks, and will gather the balls together near the top corner. All you need is a free stroke with running (left) side, playing on the left-hand side of the red about half-ball, so sending the red to bottom and side cushions and up the table after the cue ball, which makes contact on the white, either direct, after coming off the side cushion, as shown by the continuous line, or by striking one or both cushions first in the corner near the white. If you think that this is a bit "high brow," I ask you to try it and see.

Billiard and Snooker Positions

In Diagrams 27 and 28 I show the proper billiard shot followed by the proper snooker shot in the given position.

We must assume for the sake of the illustration that (*a*) is the ball "on" in the snooker shot (Diagram 28) and that the striker is not in need of any snooker, but wants to score.

The billiard shot is a cannon to get position. It must be played as lightly as possible, full on the red to send the red near the top pocket ready for in-off or pot. The other ball (*a*) is lightly doubled off side cushion towards middle of table. If you cannot do the stroke lightly with

HANDLING THE REST

single strength for this ball, (*a*) can easily be made to come off the opposite side cushion, so leaving both balls in favourable scoring positions. A good billiard player would get a nice drop cannon after going in-off the red, or he might have a cross-loser first off the spotted red after potting it, and so get both balls near the middle pocket.

For snooker, however, a slightly different angle will be taken, to double (*a*) into the opposite middle pocket. Assuming that (*b*) is the next ball to be taken, the first stroke will be played probably with stun to leave the cue ball near the position of (*a*), ready for a nearly straight pot into the "blind" corner pocket. This is not so difficult if you remember to play at moderate strength and aim just inside the further shoulder of the pocket. If you aim at the almost concealed opening of the pocket, you will probably cause the object ball to touch the nearer shoulder. Although it will bump into the pocket off the inside of the farther shoulder, a mere grazing of the nearer shoulder will keep the ball out. This applies to all such obtuse angle pots.

A snooker player who does not like the long pot into the corner, may vary his stroke here. He may put some running (left) side on the cue ball to carry it to side cushion and farther up the table towards (*b*), but the double will be made more difficult. It would be possible also to play the double with enough follow-through of the cue ball to carry it up and across the table, ready for another double on (*b*).

Using the " Bump "

Reverting to the shoulders of the pocket again, both billiards and snooker sometimes call for the use of the "bump." At the end of Diagram 29 marked (A) the cue ball is shown "angled." That is to say it cannot be played direct on either of the balls close to the cushion because the bump of the pocket is in the way. But it is easy to score a cannon by playing lightly against the opposite shoulder just where it curves outward. The cue ball will come off as shown by the line. No doubt a little practice is required before the stroke can be attempted with confidence, but that does not mean that it is very difficult.

In snooker it would only be attempted if there was nothing else to do, unless both the balls against the

(*Continued on page 88*)

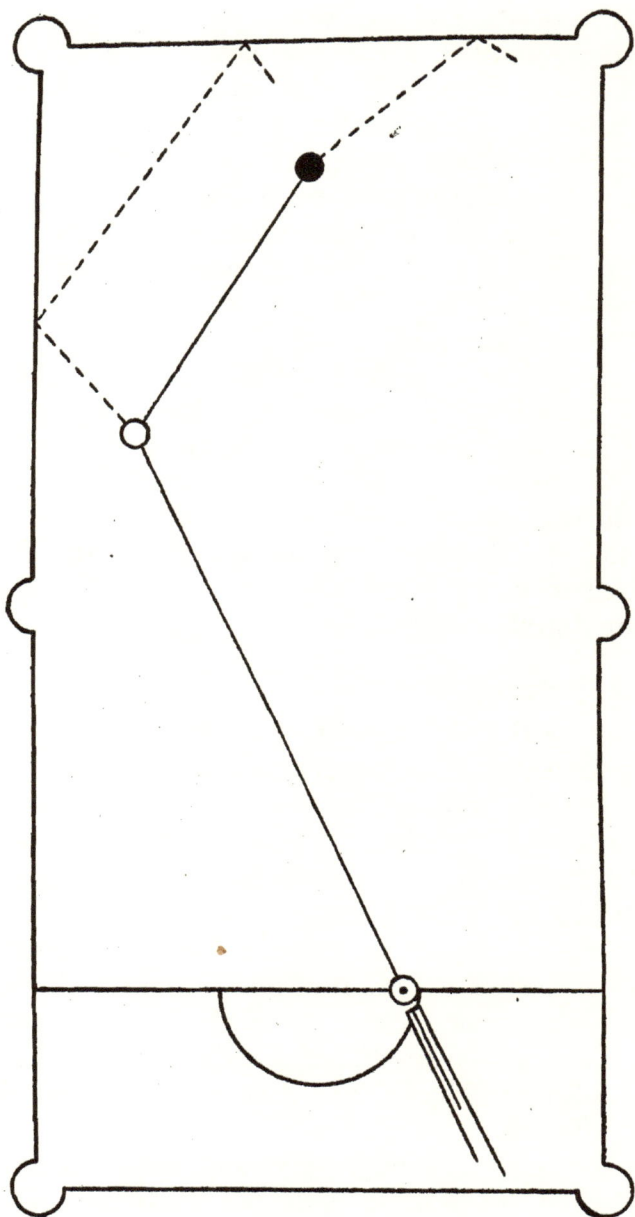

Diagram 24

DROP CANNON POSITION

Played from hand, about half-ball contact (according to precise positions of the balls), to send white and red as indicated by dotted lines, leaving a good top-of-table position. No side should be used if played from hand. No more strength than is necessary to send the white and red along dotted lines. After this stroke in billiards a series of easy shots await the careful player.

Compare this with the next diagram, for the snooker player.

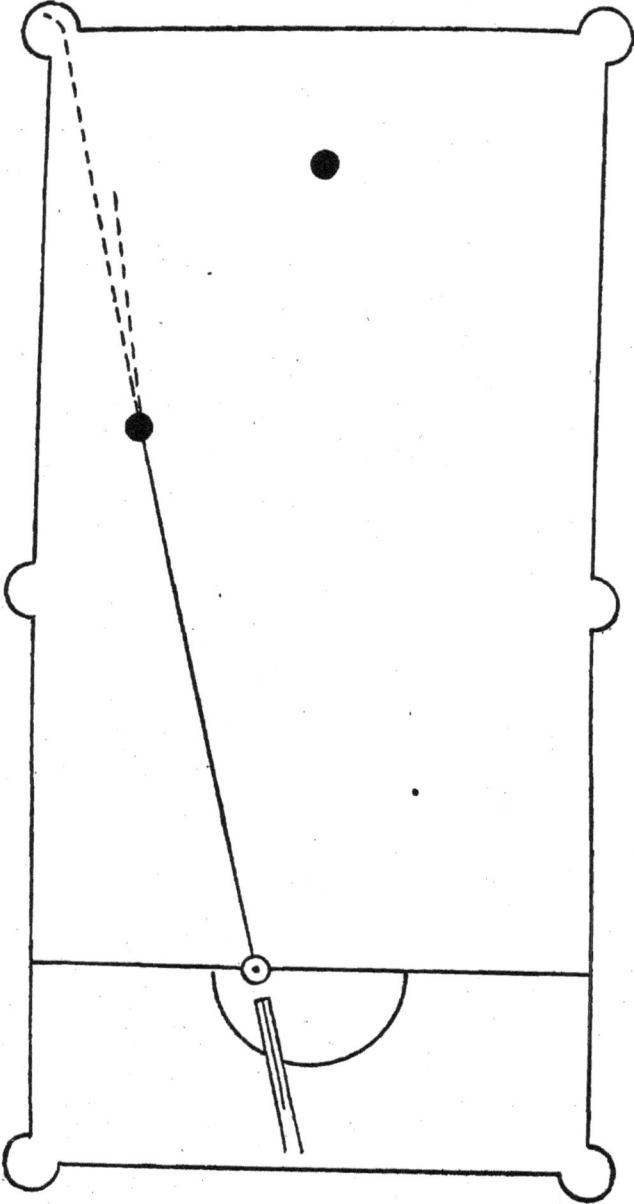

DIAGRAM 25

SNOOKER PLAY

The ball "on" is supposed to be the same as the white in the previous diagram for billiards. But play from hand being for a pot, the cue ball is placed farther along the D for a straight or nearly straight pot. The cue ball is struck a little below centre to prevent it rolling too far and spoiling position on the other ball, the black, let us say. If the cue ball is placed a little to the left of the straight pot, it will follow on slightly away from side cushion, as shown by the shorter dotted line. The same result can be achieved by using some right-hand side with a straight pot, but side will make the pot a more difficult shot.

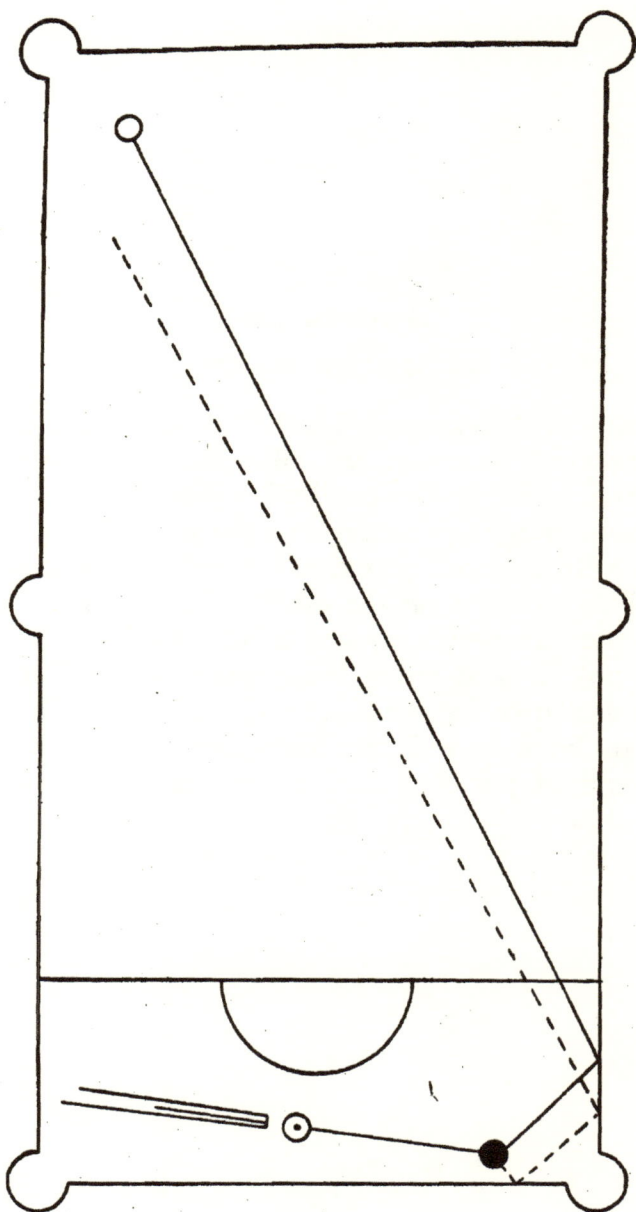

DIAGRAM 26

AVOIDING AN EASY POT IN BILLIARDS

This is a good example of the difference between billiards and snooker. Most billiard players, let alone snooker players, would pot the red in bottom pocket, and hope for the best after it was spotted on the billiards spot. But as there is very little chance of an in-off white to follow, the game is a cannon with running side, sending both balls up to the top corner. Played with a free stroke and plenty of left-hand side, it is not a difficult shot. The continuous line shows the course of the cue ball, the dotted line is the course of the object ball after being struck.

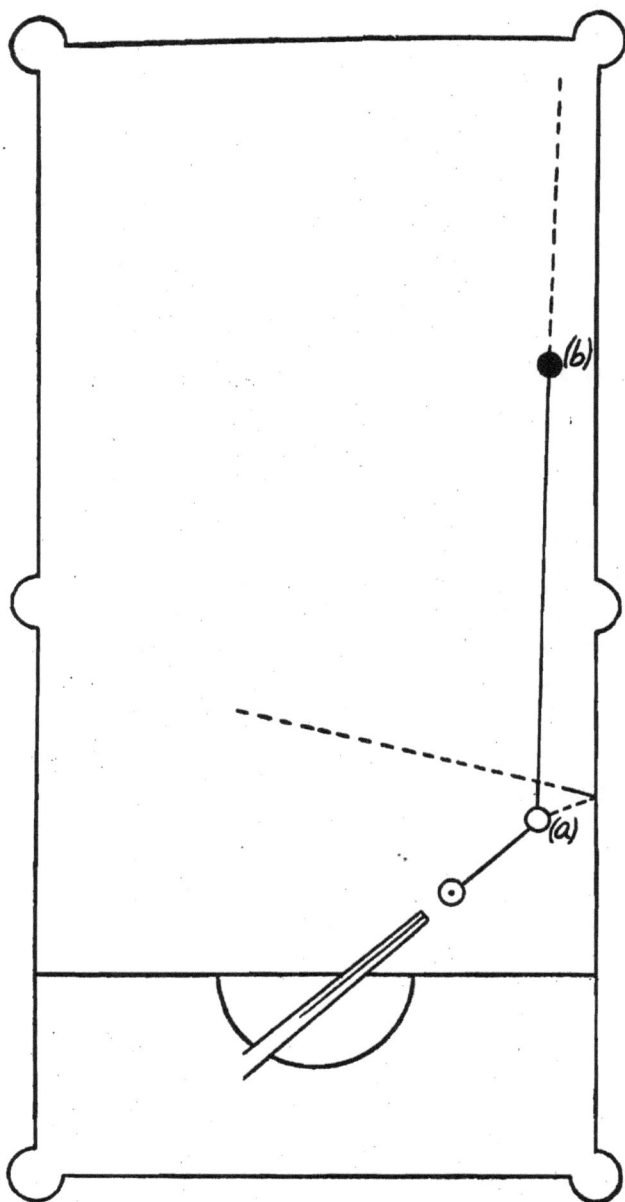

DIAGRAM 27

A BILLIARD SHOT

The proper positional shot here, if the short jenny into middle pocket is too awkward, is a soft cannon full on red, to send red up table and bring white across to middle. If the angle makes it difficult to play the stroke softly enough to stop the white going right across, play it to bring the white back off opposite cushion, being wary, of course, not to double it into the pocket. The proper angle for the cannon would not double the white into middle pocket. Compare this with the next diagram.

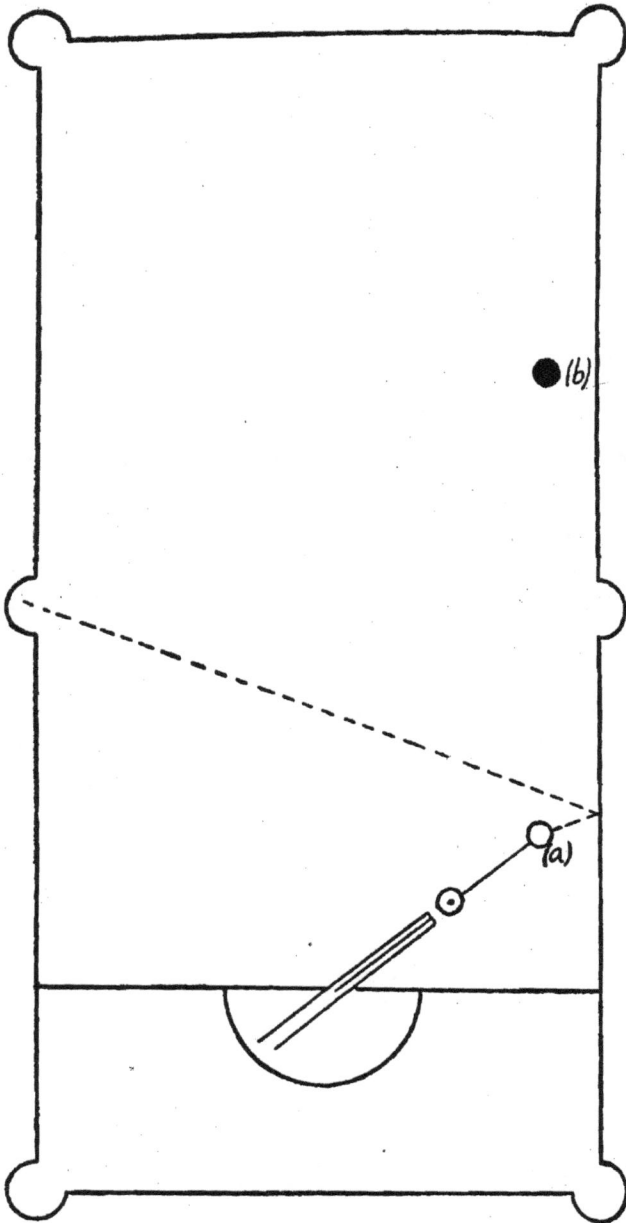

Diagram 28

A SNOOKER SHOT

With the same position as that for the billiard shot in previous diagram, the snooker shot, assuming that (*a*) is the ball "on," is to play for the double into middle pocket. If the position attracts you, a double-double, or "treble," might be done, into the opposite middle pocket. But assuming that (*b*) will be the next ball on, a double will be played with "stun" on the cue ball to keep it roughly in line with (*b*) ready for a nearly straight pot at medium to slow pace into top corner pocket. Other possible variations are referred to on p. 74. To get the double you must strike the object ball not quite full but a little to the left. "Stun" will obviate risk of a kiss. Use medium strength or less.

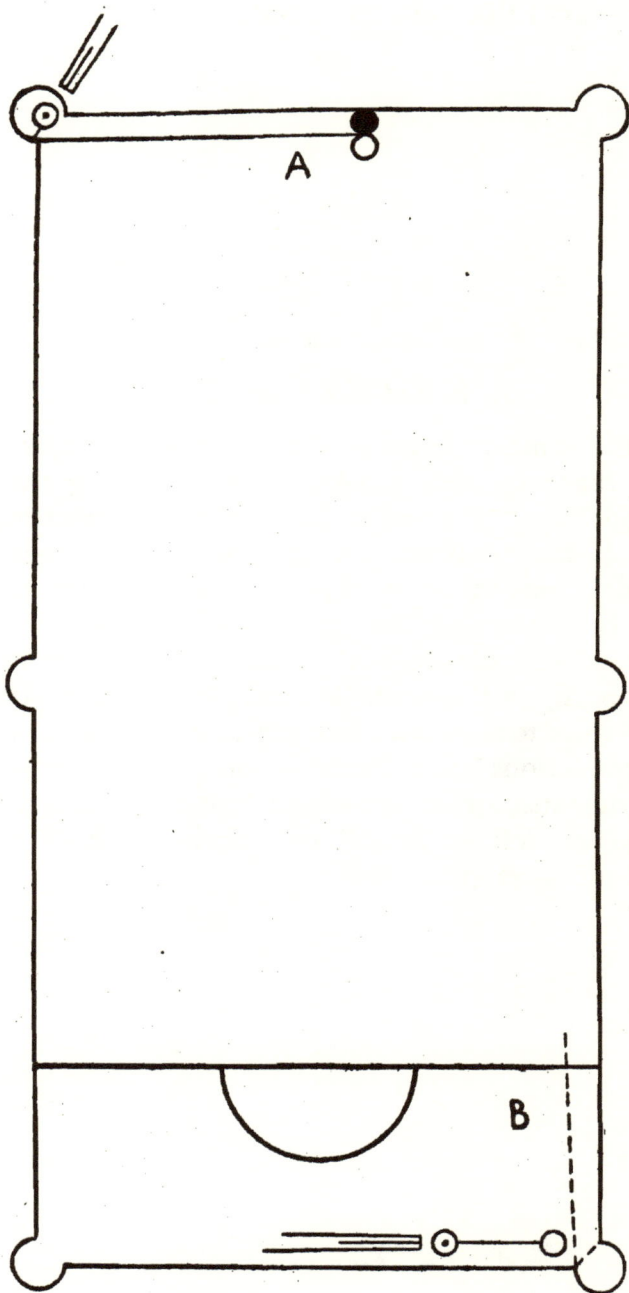

DIAGRAM 29

USING THE " BUMP "

In A, the striker being "angled" plays on the opposite "bump" of the pocket to send cue ball towards the balls that are against the cushion. This may be useful in getting out of a snooker caused by the shoulder of the pocket, or in billiards it means a useful cannon.

The shot marked B is an easy and valuable in-off when the white is blocking up the pocket. It is played to make the white strike the corner of the pocket and rebound off the opposite corner and out of the way while the cue ball follows through. Some running side (here, right) on cue ball will help to carry it into the pocket.

cushion were "on." If the one next to the cushion were a red, and the other a colour, and the striker was on a red, the shot would certainly be very difficult. Either the colour might be struck alone, or it might be struck first, or both balls might be struck simultaneously. In snooker if you strike the ball "on" simultaneously with a ball that is not the object ball, it is a foul, and you forfeit at least four points or the value of the fouled ball if this is more than four. On the other hand, not to attempt to strike the red by this means would certainly mean a free ball to the opponent, because he would not have a clear ball left on.

At the (B) end of Diagram 29 I show a purely billiard shot that makes use of the "bump." It is an in-off which many amateurs overlook, though as a shot it is less difficult than many that they habitually tackle. The knowledge of even a purely billiard stroke may be helpful to the snooker player, too. Thus if you know how the in-off is achieved, you may have better luck in avoiding it in snooker, instead of declaring that it is some demon in the cue ball which makes you give so many points away !

CHAPTER X

SPECIAL SNOOKER HINTS

I MUST assume that the reader has a general working knowledge of the game of snooker. After my previous hints on stroke play, a few suggestions as to procedure in given situations should be a help in reaching a pretty good standard.

To be dangerous at snooker a player needs to add control of position to potting ability.

Offensive-Defence

Now in my view the principal object of positional play is to facilitate scoring, though it is essential also for the negative tactics of safety. There are occasions also where a safety shot is a quick cut to scoring by compelling the opponent to leave something nice for you. We might call it offensive-defence.

In the initial stages of the game this is usually done by breaking up the red pyramid while bringing the cue ball back to the baulk end, if possible behind one of the colours there. The opponent in going for a red is likely to leave you an easy shot, or he may pot a red in one of the top pockets and get his cue ball awkwardly placed among the other reds.

Another good principle, that no professional ignores, is not to lose a chance of breaking a pack of reds when potting an isolated ball, if you have no other isolated ball well placed to follow. Sometimes this is difficult, sometimes easy, but it is an important element in scoring, especially in break building.

Breaking the Pack

Do not, as so many amateurs will do, merely smash into the pack when you are not trying to pot a particular ball. This "hope for the best" policy is likely to benefit your opponent more than yourself. Either you do not pocket a red but leave plenty on for the next player, or you may quite likely pot a red and leave the cue ball bunkered among the other reds.

At the end of this chapter I show in Diagram 30 a fairly easy and common shot which often serves me as the start of a break. Even if your break does not go on very long, at least you have given yourself a better chance of scoring than by being satisfied with a single pot.

You must judge for yourself whether the position is such that you can confidently achieve the pot, because to miss the pot and break the pack is merely to make a present to the opponent. You must be still in command of the table to benefit, and that means getting the pot you are after. In a tight game between amateurs there is much to be said for safety first and patience.

Snooker Cannons

Besides breaking a pack, as in Diagram 30, there often arises the opportunity of improving the position on the next ball by making a cannon on it—instead of on a pack of balls—when potting another. This is a more delicate stroke, perhaps, but many such situations arise, like that in Diagram 31 (A), while the same principle may be applied to safety or snooker leave, as in Diagram 31 (B). Look again also at Diagram 15 on page 46, where the use of screw for position was shown.

A cannon may seem to you to be only a billiard shot, but often the ball you want can be potted only by means of a cannon on to it, as in Diagram 32 (A). Do not, as a general rule, attempt to pot ball (*b*) here by sending ball (*a*) on to it. This is much harder than it looks and usually results in a leave for the opponent.

The Plant

But if the balls (*a*) and (*b*) are touching, of course there is a "plant," and all you need do is to strike (*a*) anywhere with the cue ball. Ball (*a*) will send (*b*) into the pocket. What you have to make sure of is that (*a*) and (*b*) make a line to the middle of the pocket, as in same diagram (B).

An exception to the general rule that you should not attempt to send one ball into the pocket by knocking another against, unless there is a "dead plant" on, is when the balls are straight along the cushion but not touching, as in Diagram 32 (C). It is fairly easy to send the first ball straight for the pocket, and if you do, it will strike the second ball true and pot it. This applies to the reds.

Potting Two Colours

It can only apply to colours when you have a free ball and the snookered ball "on" is nearest the pocket. You can always pot the snookered ball "on" while playing on your selected free ball, and you score the value of the ball "on" just as you would if you had potted the free ball. Another point about the official rules sometimes overlooked by amateurs is that there is no penalty for potting both the free ball and the snookered ball that is "on." If this happens, the ball "on" stays down, and the free ball comes up again, and you score the value of the ball "on."

When Snookered

When snookered it is sometimes undesirable or impossible to reach the snookered ball off a cushion, while a swerve shot may be fairly easy and is often much safer as regards the leave. I described the swerve shot on p. 48. In Diagram 33 (A) I show a position where you may as well play to pot the snookered ball while about it.

Never be satisfied with merely getting out of a snooker, but consider possibilities either of a score or of leaving the balls fairly safe.

Beware of playing the stroke too hard if it is one that would allow the cue ball to run far beyond the object ball. If you should miss you may easily leave another snooker, which means a free ball for your opponent.

If you yourself have a free ball and there is any choice, select one that allows you to pot and get into a good position on the next ball, that is the one that was snookered. Some players are so careless in their positional play that when they play on a free ball they leave themselves absolutely nothing to follow and may even snooker themselves.

Jump Shot

Another useful and easy stroke for getting out of a snooker is the form of the jump shot played downwards. This is much safer for the cloth than scooping the cue ball underneath, which usually is barred now in clubs and saloons. Diagram 33 (B) gives a situation where this stroke may be used. It is no use to the amateur unless the cue ball is within easy reach. The secret of the stroke is to stand well back, so that you have to stretch yourself forward, almost on your toes, your weight pressing down and forward, the bridge hand if possible on the rail, rather than on the bed of the table. The butt of the cue is raised as high as possible without altering the grip completely, the direction of aim is straight for the snookered ball, and the cue must be brought down hard on the middle of the cue ball, near the top.

By "middle" I mean precisely between the two edges, though high. The stroke differs in this, as well as in having no side, from the swerve, which involves striking downwards at the lower part of the cue ball to one side or the other. It depends how sharp the swerve must be how steeply the cue strikes down.

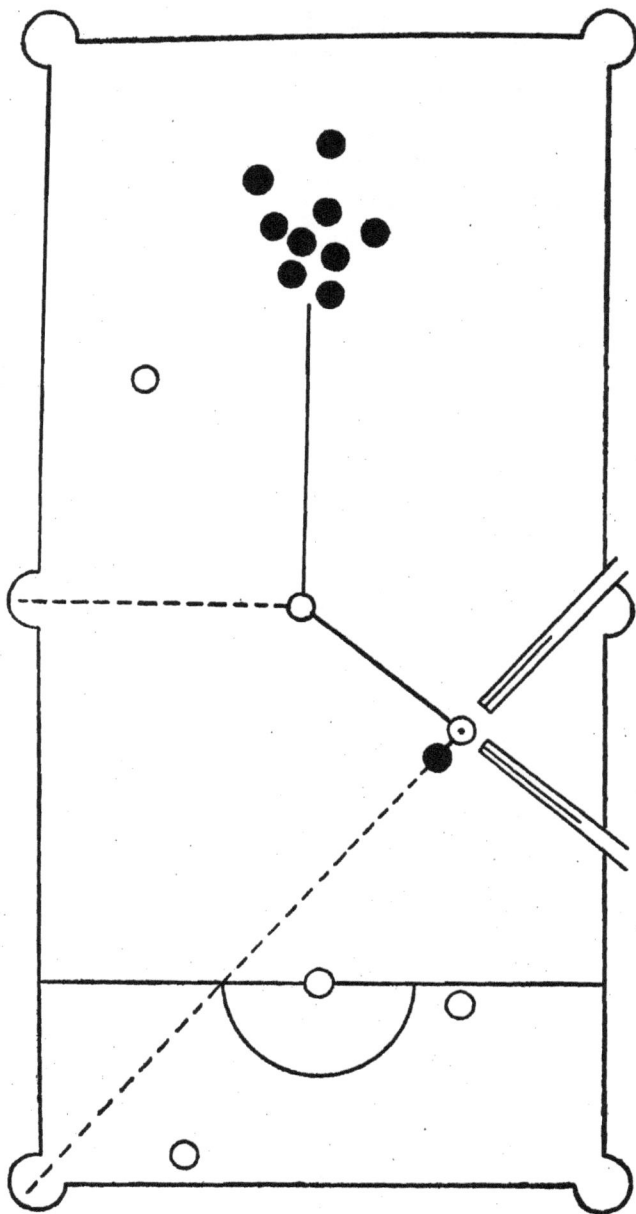

DIAGRAM 30

BREAKING THE PACK

The isolated red is first potted into left bottom pocket. Instead of allowing the cue ball to follow and then taking one of the colours in baulk, stun the cue ball to stay where you are for a pot on the blue into middle pocket. By using some screw it is easy to reach the pack with the cue ball. The straighter the pot on the blue, the more screw is wanted to bring cue ball off widely to the rack. As the shot can be done without side, there is no reason why you should miss potting the blue. Play hard enough to stir up the reds a bit.

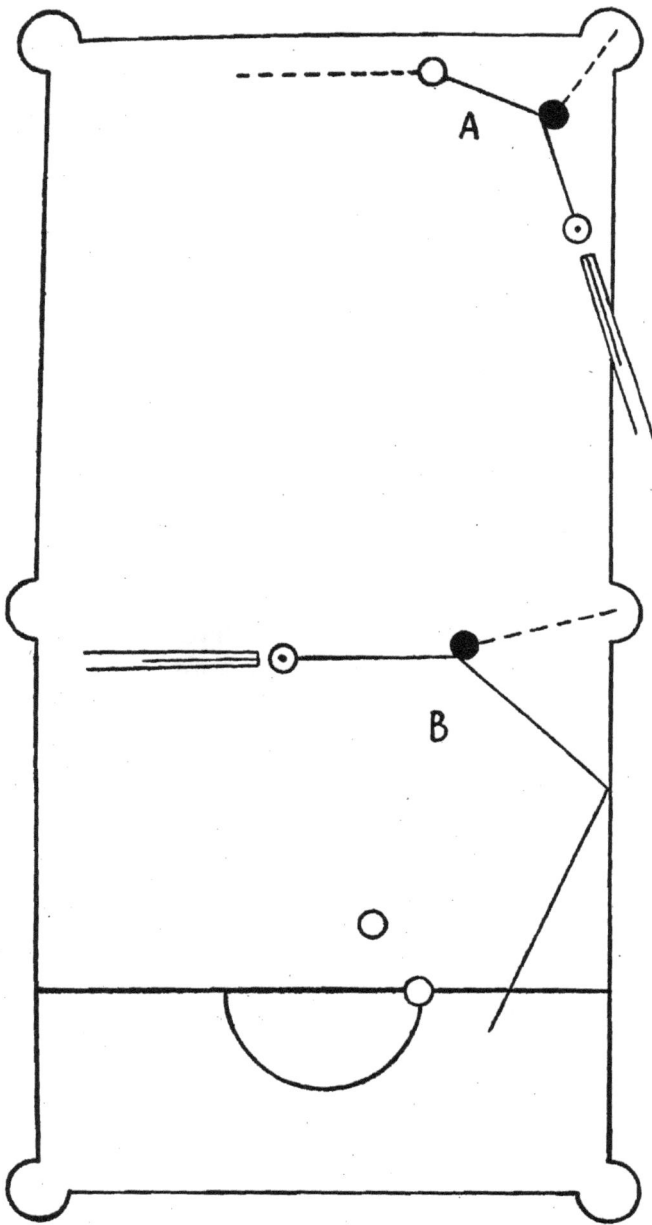

DIAGRAM 31

POSITIONAL STROKES

A. Do not be content with the pot of the red into corner pocket, but play freely, with a little screw if necessary, to cannon on the colour near top cushion, pushing this towards the other pocket, ready for the next shot.

B. Suppose that the general situation makes it desirable for you to play safe and that you can spare a red. By potting the red, you have any colour you like to play on. So instead of trying to snooker right away, pot red first, with running (right) side or some screw, to leave cue ball in baulk near the adjacent colours. Then you can give a dead snooker behind one of them for a certainty.

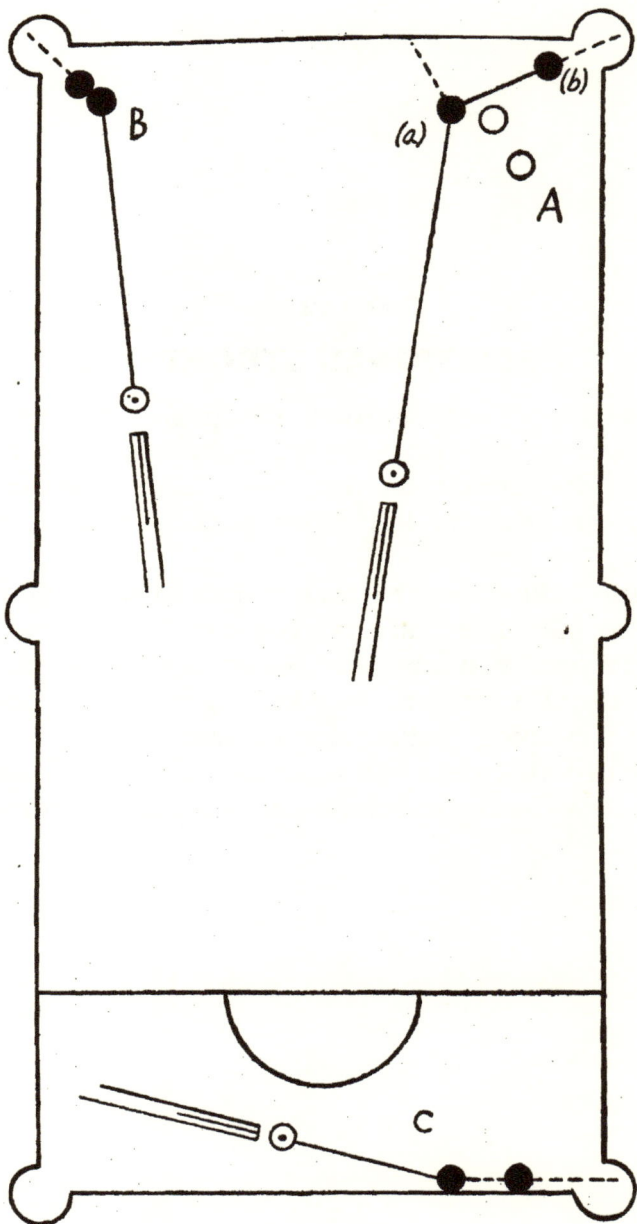

DIAGRAM 32

CANNON-POT AND PLANTS

A is a fairly easy pot of the snookered ball (*b*) by a cannon off (*a*). A little drag on the cue ball will remove the danger of going in-off after (*b*). Do not try to pot (*b*) in this position by knocking (*a*) on it. The angle is hard to judge accurately enough unless (*b*) is very close to the jaws of the pocket.

B is called a "dead plant." The two reds are touching and in a line with middle of pocket. If the first one is struck, it is bound to knock the other in.

C is a fairly easy "plant" when the balls are not touching, the cushion acting as a guide. If the first red is struck properly as it would be for a cushion pot, it will send the second red into the pocket for certain. The secret is to play on the first ball (the object ball) as if you mean to pot it. Just forget about the second ball.

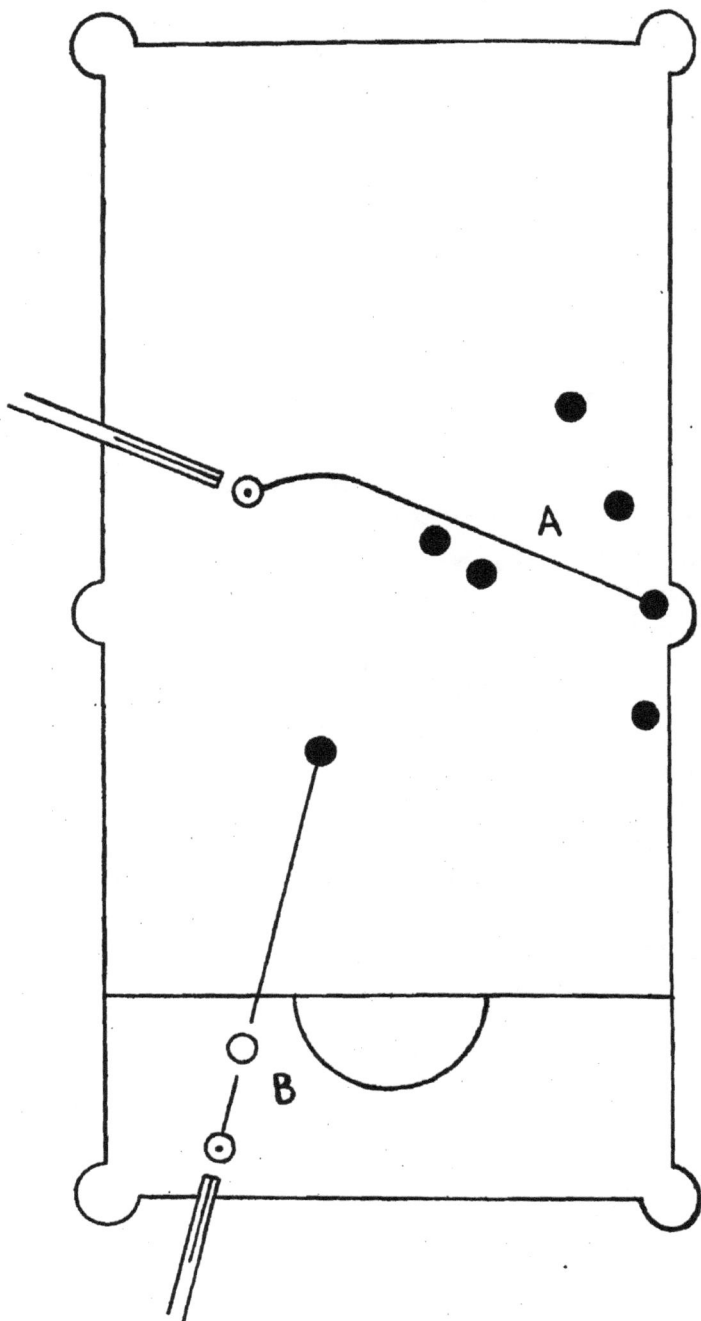

DIAGRAM 33

SWERVE AND JUMP SHOTS

A is a swerve shot on a snookered ball which has to be taken next, and in such a position the striker should not merely hit it but pot it.

B is a common situation, with cue ball in easy reach, and snookering ball at least several inches away, but not far, and not close to the object ball. The best way out of this is to jump over the obstacle and continue along the line of aim to the object ball. It does not matter how far away the object ball is. The stroke is done not by scooping up the cue ball, but by striking downwards hard on the cue ball. See page 92.

CHAPTER XI

SPECIAL BILLIARD HINTS

JUST as in snooker the cautious and dogged player may
be contrasted with the more speedy and brilliant cueist
who usually goes out for everything, so in billiards a
well contested game may be played between the quick
scorer and an opponent who tries to close the game up
with safety play, biding his time and upsetting his
opponent's chances wherever possible. A good deal of
safety play is possible in billiards, but it requires more
skill than in snooker and if it fails the consequence may
be worse than going out for scoring, and missing.

There is plenty of scope for individuality in style and
judgment as to the stroke to be played, more so than in
snooker. As safety play in general, however, covers
innumerable shots of a positional kind, most of the
subject is really covered by what I have said as to playing
your strokes correctly. The man who can do a fairly
easy shot correctly is able to play either to score or to
give a safe leave in nine cases out of ten.

Playing into Baulk

So far as safety is concerned I will refer in detail only
to baulk play. The experienced player will be familiar
with this, but for the less experienced a few hints about
giving a "double baulk" may be helpful. A single baulk
is usually desirable where the shot being attempted is
difficult and the striker thinks that if he misses it he may
let the opponent in. There is often an opportunity of
playing the shot in such a way as to leave either the cue
ball or the red in baulk, which is likely to make things

awkward for the next striker.   The best play always for scoring is the middle of the table or the top end.

If the white is out of play through being potted and you cannot continue scoring with the red with any certainty, the right game is to run both the red and the cue ball into baulk, and where this is not feasible to run one into baulk and leave the other awkwardly placed, preferably on a cushion.

The inexperienced player, however, may not realize some of the easy ways of making a double baulk from a given position.   A screw shot or a free stroke with the appropriate side may achieve this from various positions, as shown in Diagrams 34 and 35.

Top of Table Game

Probably the most worth-while sequence for break building, especially as it can be alternated with cross-losers and easy losing hazards into the middle pockets, followed by the drop cannon, is the top of the table three-ball game.   Without trying to take you into over-difficult subtleties, I show in Diagrams 36 to 38 a continuation of play from the position that followed the drop cannon shown in Diagram 24.

Assuming that the balls are aproximately placed now as in Diagram 36, the next thing to do is to pot the red and bring cue ball off side cushion round a little below the billiard spot.   The red ball now is spotted, leaving an easy cannon from red to white.   Do not pot the red here but play to send the red to side cushion near pocket and back slowly to meet the white.   The white should have been struck full and rather softly by the cue ball, causing it to just come off the top cushion.   You would then have a position with all the balls close together and ready for a series of cannons.   I realize that few amateurs could tackle this, but what any fairly good cueist should be able to do is to keep in play by having a winning hazard left when he has ruined the cannon position.

Let us suppose the situation is similar to that in Diagram 38. Then you can pot red and bring cue ball off the cushion to where a x is marked on the diagram. This leaves a second pot, with the red on the billiard spot, or, what is the proper shot, another soft cannon, this time perhaps sending the red near the corner pocket and top cushion, ready for another pot, followed by another similar cannon position.

It all depends upon whether in playing the cannon you can keep the white in position. This is done, as I have said, by making the cue ball cannon full on it, so that it goes straight to the top cushion and back, and does not finish up touching the cue ball. Anyhow, so long as you can keep the white ball near the top cushion and have a winning or losing hazard off the red, your break is not over.

You may even pot the red softly when it is near the pocket and stay there for a half-ball cross-loser into the opposite pocket, sending the red over the middle pocket, ready to be played at from baulk. Such a course is necessary if you lose position on the white.

Useful Cannons

Among the many shots for gathering the balls together when a more obvious stroke would separate them, or at least keeping a scoring position, is the type of cannon shown in Diagram 39 (A). Check side is usually wanted for such cannons, while for (B) in the same diagram, some top will assist the follow-through. The ball-cushion-ball cannon with side and the half follow-through cannon are two common and therefore important positional shots.

When you can use side and top effectively for such

shots, the rather more accurate and useful in-offs into corner pockets, by follow-through the white that is partly covering the pocket, will come fairly easily. A little practice will enable you to judge how full to strike the object ball to follow-through into the pocket

My last diagram is a favourite old curiosity, which, however, is instructive to the budding cueist who wants to get used to playing gathering shots. You would very rarely get balls precisely in the position shown in Diagram 40, but I recommend it as a simple experimental exercise to observe the behaviour of the balls, and incidentally to learn the speed of the cushions and cloth. Although this precise position is not likely to occur more than once in a blue moon, something similar may be left on at any time, and a knowledge of this easy shot will suggest a means of gathering the balls up the top end with a cannon.

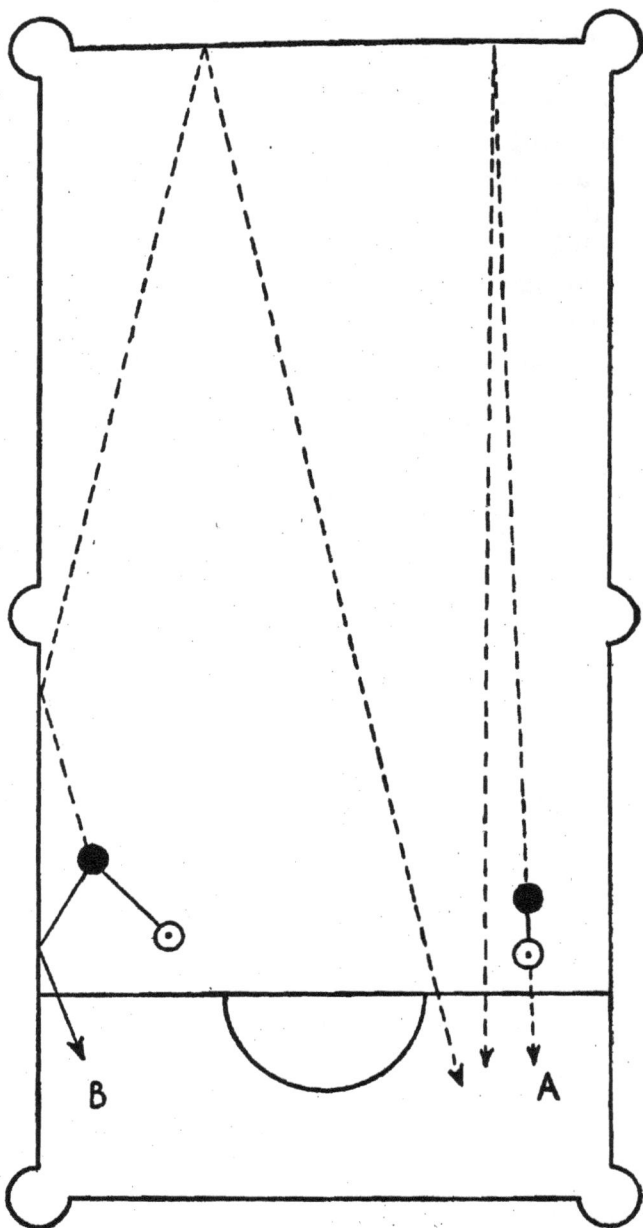

DIAGRAM 34

DOUBLE BAULK SCREW SHOTS

A is an easy straight screw back, played with enough strength to bring the other ball back off top cushion into baulk.

B is similar to many positions after white has gone out of play. There is no sure way of scoring, and the right shot is to bring both balls into baulk, the cue ball being screwed back to side cushion and into baulk, the red being driven up and down the table. The angle may allow this to be done without screwing, as shown in the next diagram.

These screw shots at the other end of the table are often useful to make a cannon on the third ball, while bringing the object ball back off the bottom cushion to the top end.

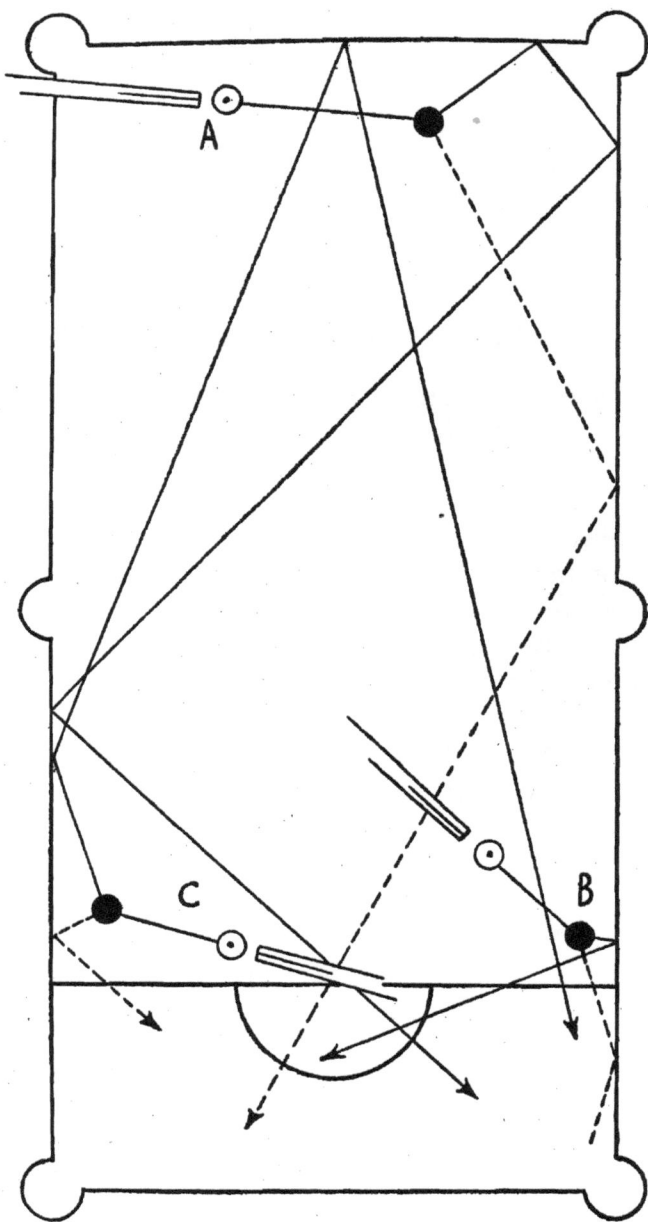

DIAGRAM 35

PLAYING INTO BAULK

A. Contact on object ball less than half-ball, to the left. Some check (left) side is advisable to bring cue ball sharply off top cushion. It follows the continuous line, the dotted line showing the course of the object ball. If the cue ball is *below* the object ball, and you still want double baulk, the shot is to strike the object ball on the *right* with running (right) side, so that the cue ball takes approximately the direction of the dotted line above, while the object ball will come off top and side cushions more or less as does the cue ball in the shot shown.

B. Using check (right) side, strike left side of object ball. The check side brings cue ball into baulk off the cushion. The shot may also be done with top instead of side, with a fairly full contact, to follow through.

C. Compare this with B in previous diagram. It is played with running side, sending cue ball up and down table, and object ball back off side cushion.

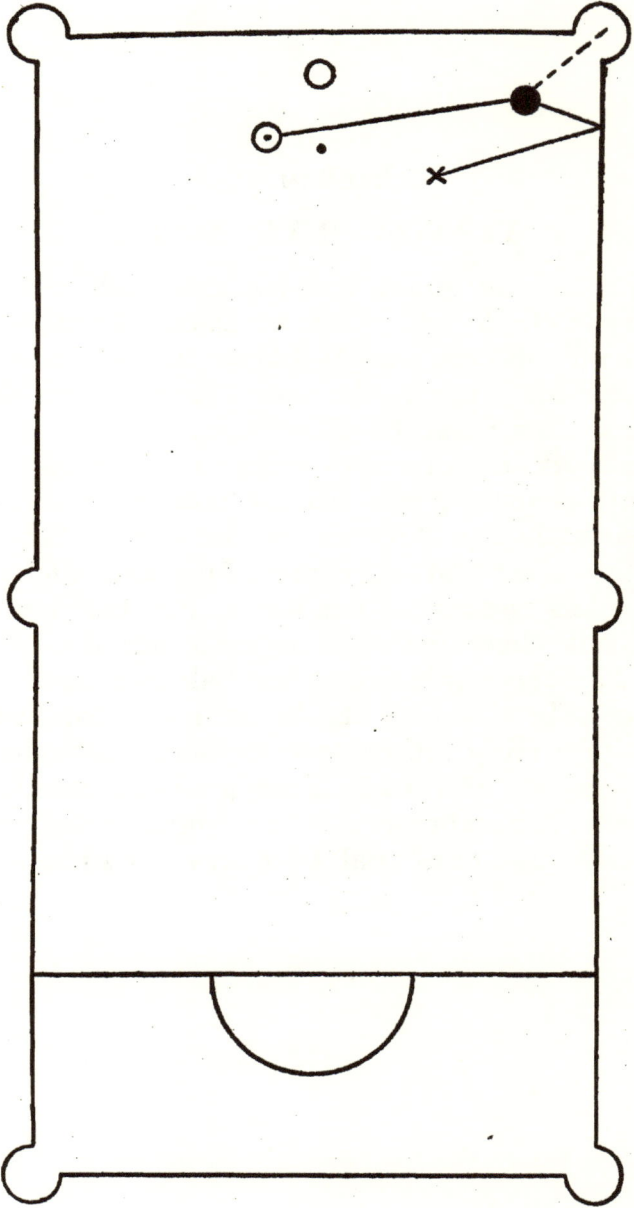

DIAGRAM 36

TOP OF TABLE SEQUENCE 2

We may count Diagram 24 as the first in this sequence, leaving the above position. You play to pot red and come round to about x, ready for the cannon shown in next diagram. The idea is always to bring the cue ball below, farther from top cushion than the billiard spot, otherwise you cannot play the cannon properly for position. Care should also be taken to keep cue ball well away from the cushion, so that your stroke is not cramped.

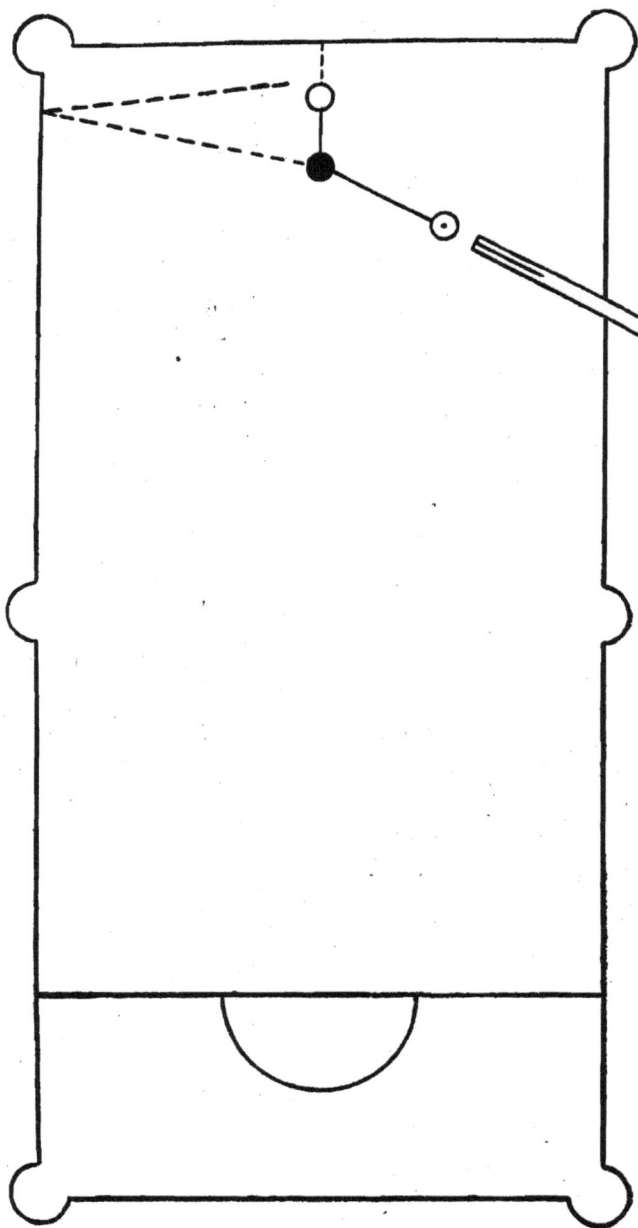

DIAGRAM 37

TOP OF TABLE SEQUENCE 3

This is the next proper shot, given the situation in the previous diagram, to cannon full on white softly and bring red back close to it, off side cushion. There should be an easy close cannon left or, if the shot is imperfect, at least a pot, provided that the white is not left touching the cue ball. After the close cannon, the red (if you cannot play a series of cannons) can be pushed over the pocket again. The situation then favours the course shown in the next diagram.

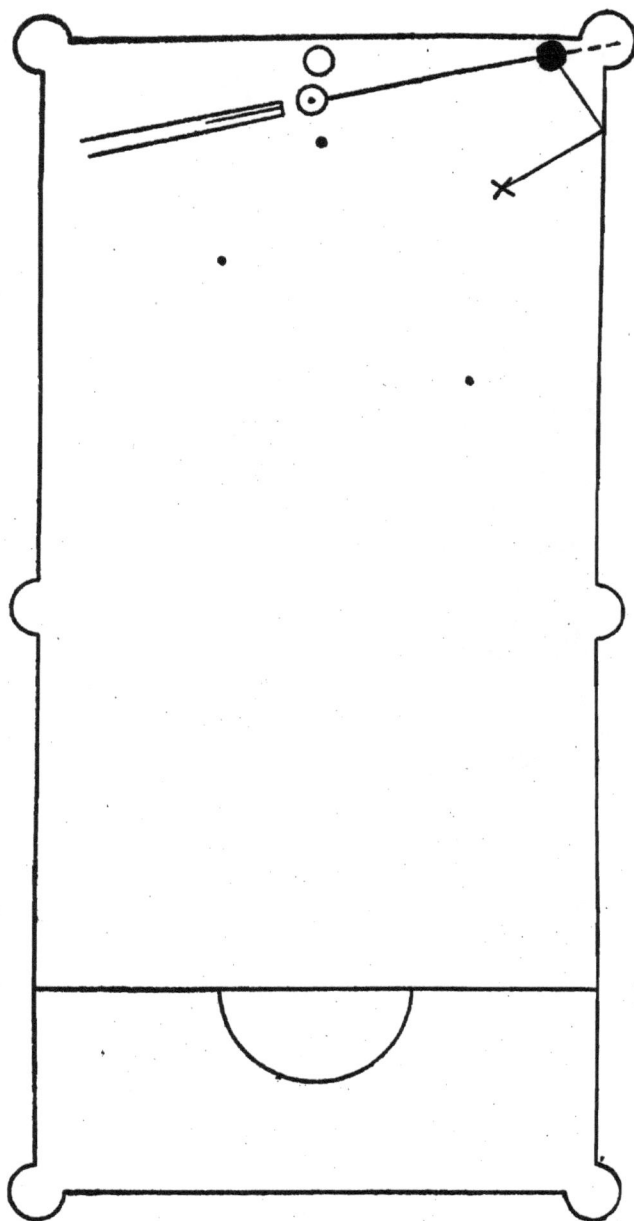

i

DIAGRAM 38

TOP OF TABLE SEQUENCE 4

This shot, properly done, roughly repeats the situation in the previous diagram. The red has been pushed near the top cushion and pocket; it is potted with a little running side on cue ball, to come back to x. Should you have lost the position of the white, so that the cannon is not convenient again, as is quite likely unless you are expert, play to pot red softly and leave cue ball in corner. A half-ball cross loser to the opposite pocket will then be on when the red is spotted, and you can carry on from in hand.

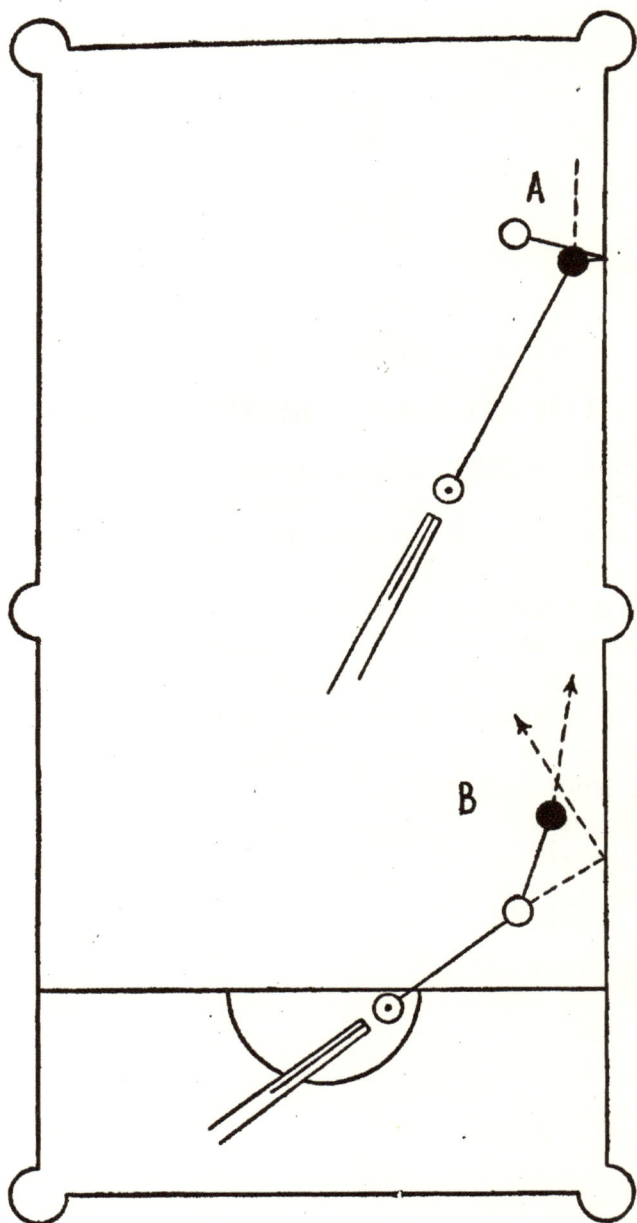

DIAGRAM 39

GATHERING CANNONS

A is a common type of cushion cannon. If the third ball is farther up the table than the object ball, as here, check (left) side is wanted to bring cue ball off the cushion at the right angle. If the balls were level, in a line parallel with top cushion, some running (right) side might be wanted. In a position like the above the tyro simply hits hard to do the cannon direct, and scatters the balls. Played as indicated the red can be pushed towards the corner pocket and the white sent a little farther up the table.

B is another cannon easy to do the wrong way, by playing it thin, or (if cue ball is in hand) from the farther end of the D. Either shot would separate the balls and leave the white badly placed. Play the cannon as a half follow-through, with top, just hard enough to send the balls near middle pocket.

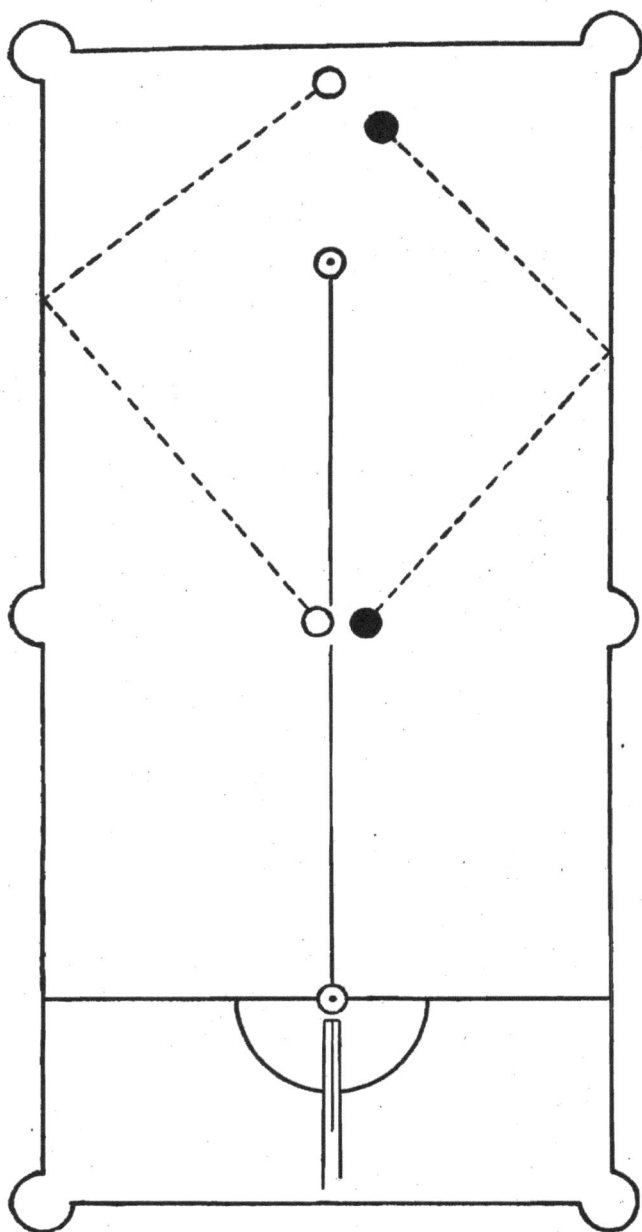

DIAGRAM 40

THE PERFECT GATHERING SHOT

Place red and white each side of the centre spot, about half a ball apart. Play from middle spot of the D without side straight up the table, with just enough strength to send the red and white to top end from the side cushions. All three balls can be easily gathered more closely than shown in the diagram. The exercise is a test of strength in the stroke. Players who feel discouraged at breaking down on their gathering shots may get a kick out of this satisfying shot! Although in actual play such a situation would be very rare, it illustrates a principle that governs many gathering shots, and may help you to use the cushions with more confidence.

PITMAN'S
GAMES AND RECREATIONS
SERIES

This is a series of books which present simply, and entertainingly the fundamentals of each sport and recreation. Written by experts they are all profusely illustrated with action photographs.

ASSOCIATION FOOTBALL. By R. T. Hesford. 8s. 6d. net.

BADMINTON. By Noel Radford. 10s. 6d. net.

BALLROOM DANCING. By Alex Moore. 10s. 6d. net.

BASKETBALL. By W. Browning. 10s. 6d. net.

BILLIARDS AND SNOOKER FOR AMATEURS. By Horace Lindrum. 6s. net.

BOWLS. By H. P. Webber and Dr. J. W. Fisher. 8s. 6d. net.

BOXING. By Thomas Inch. 10s. net.

CAMPING. By R. McCarthy. 7s. 6d. net.

CANOEING. By R. McCarthy. 12s. 6d. net.

CHESS. By C. H. O'D. Alexander. 10s. net.

THE COMPLETE CYCLIST. By Harold Moore. 7s. 6d. net.

CRICKET. By Alfred Gover. 7s. 6d. net.

FENCING. By G. V. Hett. 10s. net.

FISHING. By Ernest A. Aris. 7s. 6d. net.

GAMES AND ACTIVITIES. By Joseph Edmundson. 10s. 6d. net.

GOLF. By Charles Whitcombe. 8s. 6d. net.

HOME TRAINING FOR SPORTS AND GAMES. By Thomas Inch. 7s. 6d. net.

LAWN TENNIS. By John Olliff. 8s. 6d. net.

PHILATELY. By L. N. and M. Williams. 8s. 6d. net.

RIDING. By Lieut.-Colonel C. E. G. Hope. 7s. 6d. net.

ROWING. By G. O. Nickalls and Dr. P. C. Mallam. 10s. net.

RUGBY FOOTBALL. By Cliff Jones. 8s. 6d. net.

SAILING. By A. White. 12s. 6d. net.

SKATING WITH T. D. RICHARDSON. 12s. 6d. net.

TABLE TENNIS. By Ivor Montagu. 10s. net.

TRACK AND FIELD ATHLETICS. By D. G. A. Lowe. 8s. 6d. net.

PITMAN

BILLIARDS IN EASY STAGES

By WILLIE SMITH.

Reading this book is just like having Willie Smith standing by your elbow at the table. He immediately puts you on the right road to higher proficiency in playing billiards. Cue grip, cue bridge, stance, the use of long and short rests, the way to play different shots, and the scoring methods to employ in break-building—every point of the game is treated in detail. 3s. 6d. net.

CHESS FOR AMATEURS
How to Improve your Game

By FRED REINFELD.

This book is made up exclusively of amateurs' games. It contains a unique collection of typical errors and pitfalls, and the author's hints on how these may be avoided will be found invaluable. 7s. 6d. net.

LAWN TENNIS GUARANTEED

By EVELYN DEWHURST.

A book of practical interest to all those wishing to learn lawn tennis as well as those who desire to teach thoroughly sound, modern, methods of playing this game. Full attention is paid to footwork, drives, volleying, tactics, timing, and other important matters. Illustrations showing famous players in action are included. 15s. net.

THE BALLROOM DANCER'S HANDBOOK

By A. H. FRANKS.

An informative guide, arranged encyclopaedia wise, for the teacher and the more advanced dancer, containing all the definitions and all the different points of technique in modern ballroom dancing. 6s. net.

PITMAN